Instructor's Manual with GAMAR Disk

to accompany

Marketing Strategy
Planning and Implementation

Third Edition

Orville C. Walker, Jr.
University of Minnesota

Harper W. Boyd, Jr.
University of Arkansas – Little Rock

Jean-Claude Larréché
European Institute of Business Administration (INSEAD)

Boston   Burr Ridge, IL   Dubuque, IA   Madison, WI   New York   San Francisco   St. Louis
Bangkok   Bogotá   Caracas   Lisbon   London   Madrid
Mexico City   Milan   New Delhi   Seoul   Singapore   Sydney   Taipei   Toronto

Irwin/McGraw-Hill

A Division of The McGraw-Hill Companies

Instructor's Manual with GAMAR Disk to accompany
MARKETING STRATEGY: PLANNING AND IMPLEMENTATION

2 3 4 5 6 7 8 9 0 HAM/HAM 9 3 2 1 0 9 8

Manual ISBN 0-07-229355-1
Disk ISBN 0-07-229354-3
Package ISBN 0-256-26119-9

http://www.mhhe.com

CONTENTS

INTRODUCTION

Overall instructional strategy can follow any one of several different approaches. These include lecture-discussion, case, software, and student projects. In addition, some combination of the text readings, cases, software, and student projects can be used. This instructor's manual is designed to help you put together a teaching package of your choice. Its contents are described briefly by each of the major instructional approaches cited above.

LECTURE-DISCUSSION APPROACH:

For each chapter we have prepared a brief outline of its contents, a number of discussion questions, supplementary readings, and transparencies. In addition to these teaching aids, we list later in this section the major sources of obtaining videos and cases.

The questions on each chapter—often in the form of a mini-case—are designed to encourage high involvement and to motivate students to think about the application of concepts discussed in the text. The supplementary readings for each chapter are an effort to elaborate a given subject and in so doing help the instructor prepare lectures and/or discussion materials. The transparency masters appear in the last section of this manual. They are in black and white, and are enlargements of a select number of exhibits from the text.

VIDEOS

McGraw-Hill offers a number of videos using real world companies to illustrate certain marketing concepts and practices. For further information about these videos, contact your McGraw-Hill representative or call customer service at 1-800-338-3987.

SOURCES OF MARKETING MANAGEMENT CASE MATERIALS

Marketing management case materials can be found in a variety of sources. Many, if not most, books concerned with marketing either contain or reference such materials. This is true with general marketing management books as well as with more specialized books such as those concerned with sales management, consumer behavior, marketing research, international marketing, channels of distribution, retailing, and advertising. In addition, current articles from the journals and the business press can be used to create cases for class use. The remainder of this section is devoted to a discussion of the major sources of case material.

THE HARVARD BUSINESS SCHOOL

The largest source of marketing cases is the Harvard Business School; their 1997-98 *Catalog of Teaching Materials* devoted over 50 pages to describe an inventory of over 1,200 marketing cases. This subject area includes cases concerned with advertising, consumer marketing, industrial marketing and procurement, integrated product line management, marketing for nonprofit institutions, marketing decision support systems, marketing research, retailing, and sales management. Further, some cases developed for other subject areas (e.g., service management) may present one or more marketing issues. Such overlaps can be located in the catalog's indexes.

Each listing contains valuable information that helps in selecting a particular case for classroom use. As you will note from Exhibit 1, each entry contains the following data:

1. **Order number,** which refers to case materials only. HBS Press books, management production videos, and *Harvard Business Review* articles use different numbering systems.

2. **Product/type,** which for cases and supplements defines the main source used—field-based research, writer's general experience, secondary source materials, or published materials available to the public (such as annual reports).

3. **Author(s).** Lists the person(s) who either wrote or supervised the writing of the case.

4. **Title.**

5. **Supplementary materials.** These entries generally are listed below the entry of the item they supplement.

6. **Teaching notes.** These are not described as a separate entry. They are listed in the corresponding case entry.

7. **Source.** This denotes the source if other than the Harvard Business School.

8. **Abstract,** which describes the situation and the intended teaching purpose of the case.

9. **Setting,** which describes the geographical location of the featured company, the type of industry, the size of the company, and the year in which the situation occurred.

10. **Subject covered.** For a listing of all items on a particular subject, see the subject index.

11. **Length** (in pages) of the item and in the teaching note.

Exhibit 1

PRODUCT ENTRY ILLUSTRATION

9-293-678   Case (Gen Exp)
Bliss MC
Dillinger Bank & Trust Co. (A)
         Teaching Note (5-293-432)
Source: Stanford University
Manager Frank Fellows must decide whether to make a major
investment that would expand the trading capacity of the foreign
exchange and funding group. Company comptroller Melvin Purvis
recommends less reliance on foreign exchange trading as a source
of profits. Exhibits provide results of a certified audit performed by
Abacus CPAs. A videotape (9-893-456) provides a discussion
between Fellows and Purvis on what the branch manager's role
should be in managing the treasury side of the branch.
Setting: United States, commercial banking, $50 billion assets,
 1993
Subjects: Commercial Banking, Foreign Exchange, Investment
 Management
Length: 10p; Teaching Note: 3p

Source: Catalog of Teaching Materials 1997–1998 (Boston, MA: Harvard Business School Publishing, 1997), p. xvi.

ACCESSING CATALOG DATA

The catalog contains an annotated listing and comprehensive indexes, making it relatively easy to use. The catalog is also available on the Internet, and thus catalog users can now access information on the entire contents of the print catalog using key word searching. The catalog is updated monthly.

If you have no Internet connection, you can still search the catalog electronically using a computer disk. Users can search using key words to locate specific items. This disk has the same number of entries as the Internet catalog.

Ordering Information

Mail:	Harvard Business School Publishing Customer Service Department 60 Harvard Way Box 230-5 Boston, MA 02163
Telephone:	Inside U.S.: 800-545-7685 Outside U.S.: 617-495-6117 or 6192 (Phone lines are open 8 A.M. to 6 P.M. Eastern Standard/Daylight time)
Fax:	617-495-6985 (always open)
Internet inquiries:	Custserv@hbsp.harvard.edu

Direct Ordering and Permission Copies

You can order Harvard materials immediately with a credit card. If you are registered, you can view on screen or download full-text items (cases and *Harvard Business Review* articles). For information on these services, see the web site at http://www.hbsp.harvard.edu.

THE EUROPEAN CASE CLEARING HOUSE (ECCH)

The ECCH distributes the full case collections of INSEAD (France), IMD (Switzerland), IESE (Spain), Cranfield University(England), London Business School, Harvard Business School, The Darden School at the University of Virginia, the University of Western Ontario (Canada), and individual authors. These collections include not only case studies but videos, technical notes, industry notes, case software, and course modules. Each listing contains information that is essentially the same as that provided for the *Harvard Business School Catalog* items.

Accessing ECCH Materials

COLIS (ECCH's Case-On-Line Information System) operates through Internet and carries details of all the teaching materials developed by the sources indicated above. Each collection may be searched individually or concurrently. It is a free-text retrieval system, which allows searching on any set of characters that appear anywhere in the database. Its menu-driven searching capabilities provide easy access to this comprehensive listing of case-related materials. Access to COLIS is available over the Internet via ECCH's web site at http://www.ecch.cranfield.ac.uk. For information regarding COLIS and the procurement of ECCH materials, contact ECCH at Cranfield University or Babson College at the addresses below.

ECCH at Cranfield
Cranfield University
Wharley End
Bedford MK43 OJR England
Telephone: 44(0)1-234-7509031
FAX: 44(0)1-234-751125
E-Mail: ECCH@cranfield.ac.uk

ECCH at Babson, Ltd
Babson College
Babson Park
Wellesley, MA 02157 USA
Telephone: 617-239-5884
FAX: 617-239-5885
ECCH@Babson.edu

MARKETING MANAGEMENT CASE BOOKS:

All of the case books listed below make available an instructor's manual that contains teaching notes on all of their cases. Many of the case books offer other supplementary material, including computer assisted programs, videos, and software suggestions for case usage.

1. Kenneth L. Bernhardt and Thomas C. Kinnear, *Cases in Marketing Management* (Burr Ridge, IL: Irwin/McGraw-Hill, 1997).

2. John A. Quelch, Kamran Kashani, and Sandra Vandermerwe, *Cases in European Marketing Management* (Burr Ridge, IL: Irwin/McGraw-Hill, 1994).

3. J. Paul Peter and James H. Donnelly, Jr., *Marketing Management: Knowledge and Skills* (Burr Ridge, IL: Irwin/McGraw-Hill, 1998).

4. John A. Quelch, Robert J. Dolan, and Thomas Kosnik, *Marketing Management: Text and Cases* (Burr Ridge, IL: Irwin/McGraw-Hill, 1993).

5. David W. Cravens, Charles W. Lamb, Jr., and Victoria L. Crittenden, *Strategic Marketing Management Cases* (Burr Ridge, IL: Irwin/McGraw-Hill, 1994).

6. John A. Quelch, *Cases in Product Management*, (Burr Ridge, IL: Irwin/McGraw-Hill, 1995).

7. John A. Quelch and Paul W. Farris, *Cases in Advertising and Promotion Management* (Burr Ridge, IL: Irwin/McGraw-Hill, 1994).

8. Arthur Meidan and Luiz Mountinho, *Cases in the Marketing of Services* (Reading, MA: Addison-Wesley, 1993).

9. Roger A. Kerin and Robert A. Peterson, *Strategic Marketing Problems* (Boston, MA: Allyn and Bacon, 1997.

10. Christopher Gale, Jean-Pierre Jeannet, Kamran Kashani, and Dominique Turpin, *Cases in International Marketing* (Englewood Cliffs, NJ: Prentice Hall, 1994).

11. Linda Swann and Peter M. Ginter, *Cases in Strategic Marketing* (Englewood Cliffs, NJ: Prentice Hall, 1993).

12. Christopher H. Lovelock and Charles B. Weinberg, *Marketing Challenges: Cases and Exercises* (New York, NY: McGraw Hill, 1993).

13. Sally Dibb and Lydon Simkin, *The Marketing Case Book: Cases and Concepts* (New York, NY: Routledge, 1993). Contains a wide selection of European cases that emphasize marketing strategies and techniques.

STUDENT PROJECTS:

Such assignments can take many forms including individual versus group reports, written versus oral presentations (or both), loosely versus highly structured reports, industry versus company specific assignments, library versus field research, and so on. Examples of possible topics or subject areas for such projects are listed below. They should be applicable to a variety of project types.

I. Evaluating corporate and business strategies of a specific company. This can be accomplished through library and/or field research. The presentation—after describing the nature and scope of the company—should ideally address the following subject areas.

   A. Environmental trends affecting the industry and their relative importance.

   B. How these trends are and will impact the firm being studied and its close competitors.

   C. An analysis of individual close competitors including how they constrain the activities of the company under investigation.

   D. The company's corporate strategy—especially with respect to its SBU portfolio.

E. The business strategy for one of the company's SBUs and the implications of this strategy for marketing.

F. The target audience for a given product-market entry and how it is positioned including an evaluation of its positioning strategy.

G. An evaluation of the firm's product-market entry's marketing plan.

H. Suggestions on what changes are needed to improve the entry's performance and cope with industry trends.

II. Individual subject area reports/presentations

A. Economic/demographic trends and what opportunities and threats they pose. The implications of these trends can be discussed in general, as they impact a specific industry, or as they affect a given company.

B. Regulatory actions affecting business strategies and marketing planning.

C. Social trends affecting buyer behavior, thereby providing opportunities for, and threats to, some companies and their products.

D. Conducting an industry analysis for a specific industry and "predicting" the future bases of competition for firms within a given strategic group.

E. Technological trends and their affect on a given industry and the kinds of company resources required for success.

F. The government regulations concerning a firm's promotional activities and how this affects a firm's strategy formulation and execution.

G. A discussion of the most important segmentation variables for market targeting.

H. A case study involving the positioning of a new consumer product, a new industrial product, a new consumer service.

I. Changing marketing organizational structures and their implications for developing and executing business strategies.

III. Developing a marketing plan for a new product or service. The plan should contain the following.

A. The benefits/attributes of the product or service.

B. Description of the intended market.

C. An analysis of the various environmental factors which will affect the industry and, in turn, the companies comprising it.

D. A discussion of the product's positioning including how it relates to presumed market needs and competitive products.

E. The marketing mix to be used (describe the company's pricing, distribution, and promotion activities).

F. What kinds of information does the company need to monitor how well the product is being marketed—and how (where) can such information be obtained?

IV. Developing an international marketing plan. In an effort to make students more aware of the difficulties associated with global marketing, have students select and research a foreign country's environment—especially with reference to the following subject areas.

A. A brief history of the country or culture.

B. Demographic/economic characteristics.

C. Political/legal business constraints.

D. Social customs/family influences.

E. Infrastructure; e.g., communication systems, roads, transport/storage facilities/ organizations, security, business statistics, and relevant channels of distribution.

F. Major industries/companies and level of economic development.

G. Skills of the relevant labor force.

H. Relevant societal customs and values.

The above information should be used to develop recommendations for conducting business in this country for a company of a student's choice.

CHAPTER 1
THE STRATEGIC ROLE OF MARKETING

I. COMPAQ SHIFTS STRATEGIES

    A. Changing customer demands and competitor actions lead to a shift in strategy

    B. New corporate and competitive strategies

    C. New strategic marketing programs

    D. The bottom line

II. CORPORATE, BUSINESS AND MARKETING STRATEGIES—DIFFERENT ISSUES AT DIFFERENT ORGANIZATIONAL LEVELS

    A. Strategy: a definition

    B. The components of strategy

    C. The hierarchy of strategies

    D. Corporate strategy

    E. Business-level strategy

    F. Marketing strategy

III. STRATEGIC PLANNING SYSTEMS

    A. The value of formal planning systems

    B. Evolution of planning systems

        1. Financial planning systems

        2. Long-range planning systems

        3. Strategic planning systems

        4. Strategic management systems—tools for creating market-driven strategies

    C. Characteristics of effective planning systems

IV. THE ROLE OF MARKETING IN FORMULATING AND IMPLEMENTING STRATEGIES

    A. Factors that mediate marketing's role in strategic planning

        1. Market-oriented management

        2. Competitive factors affecting a firm's market orientation

3. The influence of different stages of development across industries and global markets

4. Strategic inertia

B. Recent developments affecting the strategic role of marketing

1. Globalization

2. Increased importance of service

3. Information technology

4. Relationships across functions and firms

C. The future role of marketing

V. THE PROCESS OF FORMULATING AND IMPLEMENTING MARKETING STRATEGY

A. Interrelationships among different levels of strategy

B. Market opportunity analysis

1. Environmental, industry, and competitor analysis

2. Customer analysis—segmentation, targeting, positioning

C. Formulating strategies for specific market situations

D. Implementation and control

VI. SUMMARY

ANSWERS TO DISCUSSION QUESTIONS

1. **What are the critical issues that should be addressed at each of the following levels of strategy?**

   a. **Corporate strategy**

   b. **Business-level (SBU) strategy**

   c. **Marketing strategy**

Level of Strategy	*Critical Issues*
Corporate	• What is the firm's mission or strategic intent? • What is the company's strategic domain—what businesses should it be in? • What direction will the firm take in the pursuit of future growth and development? • What portion of total resources should the company devote to each of its businesses to achieve its overall goals and objectives? • What resources, technologies and/or functional competencies should be shared across businesses in order to achieve synergies?
Business-level	• How should the business compete in its industry? How will it gain and sustain a competitive advantage? • What is the business' domain? What product-markets should it focus upon? • How should the business' resources be allocated across those product-markets to achieve the business' objectives? • What resources or competencies should be shared across product-markets to achieve synergy?
Marketing	• What segments exist within a given market? • Which of those segments should be targeted? • How should the product offering be positioned in each target market relative to customer needs and competitive offerings? • How should resources be allocated across the components of the marketing program in each target market?

2. **How are the basic business philosophies or orientations of a major consumer products firm like General Mills and a small, entrepreneurial start-up in a fast-growing, high-tech industry likely to differ? How are the planning processes used by the two firms likely to differ? What are the implications of such philosophical and procedural differences for the role of marketers in the strategic planning conducted within the two firms?**

Due to the maturity, slow growth rate, and competitiveness of General Mills' market environment, the firm is likely to have a strong market orientation characterized by: (a) efforts to understand changing customer needs, (b) the development of quality products and marketing programs tailored to those needs, and (c) cross-functional coordination and involvement in satisfying customers. The firm's size and the complexity of its many businesses also suggest it is likely to have a more highly evolved, "bottom-up" planning system—probably of the "strategic planning" or "strategic management" type—to enable faster and more innovative responses to rapidly developing threats and opportunities. All of this indicates that marketing personnel are likely to play an extensive role in collecting and analyzing consumer and competitor information, and in helping develop strategic plans at both the business and product-market levels.

Given that a small, high tech start-up firm is likely to face many technical and operational problems due to technological uncertainties, rapid growth, and limited resources, such a company is more likely to be technically and production oriented. Similarly, its small size, limited human and financial resources, and early stage of development are more likely to be associated with a rather simple, top-down planning system—probably focused primarily on financial planning and budgetary control. Consequently, such a firm is unlikely to have a very extensive marketing department (although it may rely heavily on a more narrowly-focused sales function), and marketing's role in strategic planning is probably limited.

3. **As the small entrepreneurial firm described in question #2 grows larger, and its industry matures and becomes more competitive, how are (or should) its business philosophy and planning processes likely to change? Why?**

The firm is likely to move from a production- to a sales- and, perhaps, finally, to a market-orientation. It is also likely to move toward a more extensive, flexible, and decentralized planning system. As the industry matures, technological change and sales growth rates are likely to slow, and new competitors will enter. As product differentiation narrows and excess capacity develops within the industry, the firm will probably engage in more aggressive selling activities aimed at moving available stocks. If the firm survives the industry shakeout period, it may become more customer-oriented and decentralized in order to respond to more specialized market needs and to find new ways to gain an advantage over its competitors.

4. **What role should marketing managers play in helping to formulate business-level (SBU) strategies in a large diversified firm like General Electric? What kinds of information are marketers best able to provide as a basis for planning? What issues or elements of business-level strategy can such information help to resolve?**

    Since marketing managers occupy positions at the boundary between the company and its customers and competitors in the market, they should play a central role in collecting and analyzing customer and competitor information, defining market segments, and tracking relevant environmental trends, threats, and opportunities. As a result, they are well qualified to play a major role along with the Business Unit manager in defining the business' scope (e.g., target markets and product offerings), objectives, and competitive strategy. They should also have a major role in considerations of the business' directions for future growth, new product and market development efforts, and efforts to improve product and service quality.

SUPPLEMENTARY REFERENCES

See Footnotes 2, 4, 9, 15, 18

TRANSPARENCIES:

Chapter exhibits for which transparency masters prepared: 1, 2, 3, 6, 8

CHAPTER 2
CORPORATE STRATEGY DECISIONS

I. GILLETTE—AN INNOVATIVE GLOBAL COMPETITOR

    A. Gillette's corporate mission and strategic scope

    B. Gillette's corporate objectives and development strategy

II. STRATEGIC DECISIONS AT THE CORPORATE LEVEL

III. CORPORATE SCOPE: DEFINING THE FIRM'S MISSION AND INTENT

    A. Factors that influence the corporate mission

        1. Social values and ethical principles

        2. Internal resources and competencies

        3. Opportunities and threats

    B. Dimensions for defining the corporate mission

    C. Strategic intent or vision: a motivational view of the corporate mission

IV. CORPORATE OBJECTIVES

    A. Enhancing shareholder value: the ultimate objective

    B. Most organizations pursue multiple objectives

    C. Business-unit and product-market objectives

V. CORPORATE DEVELOPMENT STRATEGY

    A. Expansion

        1. Market penetration

        2. Product development

        3. Market development

    B. Diversification

        1. Vertical integration

        2. Related diversification

        3. Unrelated diversification

        4. Diversification through organizational relationships or networks

VI. ALLOCATING CORPORATE RESOURCES

    A. Portfolio models

        1. The Boston consulting group's (BCG) growth-share matrix

        2. Resource allocation and strategy implications

        3. Limitations of the growth-share matrix

        4. Alternative portfolio models

    B. Value-based planning

        1. Discounted cash flow model

        2. Some limitations of value-based planning

VII. SOURCES OF SYNERGY

VIII.   SUMMARY

ANSWERS TO DISCUSSION QUESTIONS

1. **When Toyota began development of the Lexus automobile to compete in the luxury car market against such firms as BMW and Mercedes Benz, the firm's rallying cry was "Beat Benz!" What are the advantages and limitations of such an emotional statement of strategic intent?**

   Such statements of strategic intent are more general than typical mission statements, but they tend to be more personally motivating because they appeal to employees' competitive instincts and desires for accomplishment. While they should be clear about the firm's long-term ends, they also tend to be flexible as to means. Thus, there is room for innovation and employees' are encouraged to make the most of available resources, be inventive, and develop new capabilities.

   The risk is that there may be many different means of pursuing a given strategic intent, and some of those means may be inconsistent or complete with one another. Thus, even a clear statement of intent may not be specific enough to focus efforts and avoid the dissipation of energy and resources. To overcome such problems, some firms combine a statement of strategic intent with a more traditional mission statement in order to focus efforts on a more clearly defined domain of customer needs and product-markets. Another approach is to break down a broad statement of strategic intent into a series of shorter-term goals that need to be accomplished for the intent to be realized.

2. **A manufacturer of electrical components for industrial applications has the five strategic business units (SBUs) shown in the following table. Using the Boston Consulting Group portfolio model, evaluate the strength of the company's current and potential future position. What strategies should it consider to improve its future position?**

SBU	Dollar Sales (in millions)	Number of Competitors	Dollar Sales of Top 3 Competitors (in millions)			Market Growth Rate
A	1.0	7	1.4,	1.4,	1.0	15%
B	3.2	18	3.2,	3.2,	2.0	20%
C	3.8	12	3.8,	3.0,	2.5	7%
D	6.5	5	6.5,	1.6,	1.4	4%
E	.7	9	3.0,	2.5,	2.0	4%

15

An approximation of the BCG growth-share matrix for this situation is shown below. Note that relative market share is determined by dividing the company SBUs sales volume by that of the next largest competitor.

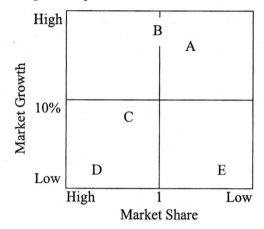

One implication is that funds from the "cash cows" SBUs (D and C) should be used to fund efforts aimed at increasing the relative market shares of the "question mark" SBU (A) and the borderline SBU (B) in order to move them into the "star" category. This is essential for future profitability because, as stars, those businesses will become the firm's cash cows as their growth rates slow. If they are allowed to remain question marks, however, they will decline into "dogs" in the future. Unfortunately, this analysis says nothing about *how* the firm might best be able to improve the relative shares of D and C. Nor does it give any clues about where new question mark or star businesses might come from in the future.

Because business E has a very low market share in a slowly growing market, some consideration might be given to divesting or harvesting that business.

3. **Critics argue that the BCG portfolio model sometimes provides misleading advice concerning how resources should be allocated across SBUs or product-markets. What are some of the possible limitations of the model? What might a manager do to reap the benefits of portfolio analysis while avoiding at least some shortcomings you have identified?**

Limitations of the BCG growth-share matrix include:

- Inadequacy of growth as an indicator of industry attractiveness
- Inadequacy of relative market share as an indicator of overall competitive strength
- Sensitivity to variations in possible measures of "growth" and "share"

16

- Difficulty in determining the appropriate definition of the relevant market (e.g., market may be defined at too aggregate a level and include too many product types and/or customer segments)
- Lack of guidance concerning how appropriate investment strategies should be implemented

Some of these problems can be at least partially overcome by using more detailed portfolio models which incorporate multiple variables to evaluate market attractiveness and competitive strength. Regardless of which model is used, however, it should be considered as only one of a set of complementary analytical tools. Such models should be used in conjunction with other techniques (e.g., value-based planning) and a substantial amount of management judgement and common sense within the strategic planning process.

4. **Value-based planning has gained acceptance within many companies as a tool for evaluating alternative business strategies and thereby helping to make resource allocation decisions within a business. What are some of the advantages of value-based planning that have made it attractive to so many firms? What are some of its major limitations?**

Value-based planning attempts to overcome one of the weaknesses of portfolio models by providing more guidance concerning the most appropriate means for investing or harvesting funds in a particular business. It is a tool for assessing the shareholder value that a given competitive strategy is likely to create over the course of a planning period. Thus, it provides a basis for comparing the economic returns to be gained from investing in different businesses pursuing different strategies, or from alternative strategies that might be adopted by a given business unit. Thus, the technique was particularly appealing to corporate managers who feared that low returns to shareholders might lead to a takeover hostile acquisition attempts. Value-based planning is also consistent with other managerial tools and actions aimed at improving the "Economic Value Added" (EVA) of a firm and its constituent business units.

The major limitations of value-based planning mostly involve problems in estimating important underlying variables, including the following:

- Difficulty in estimating the business' risk-adjusted cost of equity capital
- Difficulty in predicting the "residual value" that will be produced by a given strategy after the planning period is over
- Problems in estimating the "prestrategy" value (i.e., the value that would be produced by the business' current strategy if no changes are made)

In addition, value-based planning can only evaluate alternatives that have already been developed by managers. Thus, it should be considered as only one tool to be used as part of a more detailed and inventive strategic planning process.

SUPPLEMENTARY REFERENCES:

See Footnotes 6, 17, 19, 21, 23, 37

TRANSPARENCIES

Chapter exhibits for which transparency masters prepared: 1, 3, 7, 7, 8, 9, 10, 11

CHAPTER 3
BUSINESS STRATEGIES AND THEIR MARKETING IMPLICATIONS

I.   BUSINESS STRATEGIES AND MARKETING PROGRAMS AT 3M

II.   THE CONCEPT OF STRATEGIC FIT

III. STRATEGIC DECISIONS AT THE BUSINESS-UNIT LEVEL

    A. Defining strategic business-units

    B. Business-unit objectives

    C. Allocating resources within the business unit

    D. The business unit's competitive strategy

    E. Business-level strategies for global competitors

IV. THE UNDERLYING DIMENSIONS OF ALTERNATIVE BUSINESS STRATEGIES

    A. Differences in scope

    B. Differences in goals and objectives

    C. Differences in resource deployments

    D. Differences in sources of synergy

V.   THE FIT BETWEEN BUSINESS STRATEGIES AND THE EXTERNAL ENVIRONMENT

    A. Appropriate conditions for a prospector strategy

    B. Appropriate conditions for an analyzer strategy

    C. Appropriate conditions for a defender strategy

        1. Differentiated defenders

        2. Low-cost defenders

    D. Changing strategies at different stages in the industry life cycle

VI. MARKETING IMPLICATIONS OF DIFFERENT BUSINESS STRATEGIES

    A. Product policies

    B. Pricing policies

ANSWERS TO DISCUSSION QUESTIONS

1. **The 3M Company's Industrial Tape SBU pursues a differentiated defender strategy in an industry where both the basic technologies and the customer segments are relatively mature and stable. Is the objective—imposed by top management—of obtaining 30 percent of sales from products introduced within the last four years an appropriate objective for such an SBU? What do you think top management hopes to accomplish by imposing such an objective on the Industrial Tape SBU? What are the potential disadvantages or dangers involved in imposing such an objective?**

Aggressive new product development and volume growth objectives are typically not very appropriate for defender SBUs operating in relatively mature markets. Such businesses usually perform better on financial dimensions—such as ROI and cash flow—than on growth dimensions.

Because skills in R&D and new product development are among 3M's greatest competitive strengths, management imposed it "30 percent of sales from new products" objective on all divisions to motivate them to maintain and build upon those competencies. The objective also motivates SBU managers to aggressively seek growth from new applications and new markets based on product improvements and line extensions.

The potential dangers in this approach are that defender divisions will spend an inordinate amount of time and money developing "new" products that represent only marginal changes from existing products and that contribute little additional volume. Worse, they may develop new products that cannibalize more profitable old products. In either case, the risk is that economies of scale and experience may be lost and expenses (e.g., R&D and marketing costs) as a percent of sales will increase, with a resulting reduction in financial performance.

2. **Suppose you have been the marketing manager for 3M's Industrial Tape SBU (as described in question #1 above). You have just been informed that you are being transferred to a similar position within the company's Health Care SBU; a business unit that pursues a prospector strategy aimed at the rapid development of new products for newly emerging markets. Would you see the transfer as a positive step in the development of your career? How are your responsibilities and your decision making influence likely to change as a result of the transfer?**

For a marketing manager, such a transfer would probably be considered as a positive move. Issues related to operating efficiency and effectiveness are crucial for defender businesses (e.g., process R&D, manufacturing, distribution, etc.), and their focus tends to be on financial rather than growth objectives. Consequently, marketing concerns may be somewhat secondary and marketing managers often play less central roles in making strategic and operating decisions in such businesses. On the other hand, prospectors focus on attaining growth through new product and market development. Consequently, marketing and marketing research activities (together with R&D) are critical to the success of such businesses and marketing managers are likely to play a more central role in their strategic decision making process.

3. **You are the marketing vice president for Minnetonka, Inc., a small firm whose success is dependent on pioneering the development of new personal care products such as Softsoap and Check-Up toothpaste. What areas of functional competence are critical for the continued success of such a business? As marketing vice president, what role would you and your subordinates play in determining the firm's future success?**

While general management skills are important for a business' success regardless of the competitive strategy being employed, competence in product R&D, marketing, market research, and sales are especially critical for the success of a prospector business. Besides the obvious need for competence in identifying market opportunities and developing innovative new products, skills in advertising and consumer promotion are important for winning customer adoption of those new products, and skills in trade promotion and selling to large retailers are needed to gain adequate distribution for a constant stream of new offerings.

Because Minnetonka was a small single-business firm, skills in raising funds and financial management were also quite important for keeping pace with rapid growth.

4. **You are the marketing manager for the generic products division of a major pharmaceutical manufacturer. Your division uses the corporation's excess manufacturing capacity to produce generic prescription drugs—drugs whose patents have expired and can thus be manufactured by any company that wishes to produce them. Your division is a low cost defender that maintains its position in the generic drug market by holding down its cost and selling generic products to distributors and pharmacies at very low prices. What are the implications of this business strategy for each of the "4 Ps" in the strategic marketing program you would develop for your division?**

As a low cost defender who competes primarily by offering the lowest prices, the business must strive to minimize its costs in as many areas as possible. Its focus on selling only existing products that have lost their patent protection (thus avoiding R&D costs) and relying on excess production capacity available in the corporation (rather than investing in dedicated facilities) is consistent with its strategy. In addition to minimizing marketing costs associated with product development or improvement activities, it should largely avoid consumer advertising and promotion (although some primary demand advertising might be aimed at encouraging consumers to request generic drugs from their pharmacist rather than paying more for brand name prescription drugs). Some trade promotion and personal selling effort will have to be focused on encouraging distributors and pharmacists to stock and sell the firm's generics rather than competing products, but those costs should be controlled as tightly as possible.

SUPPLEMENTARY REFERENCES:

See Footnotes 1, 6, 8, 9, 10, 13, 16, 22

TRANSPARENCIES:

Chapter exhibits for which transparency masters prepared: 2, 4, 6, 7, 8, 9

CHAPTER 4
ENVIRONMENTAL ANALYSIS

I.   DANGEROUS ROAD AHEAD FOR AMERICA'S AUTOMOTIVE INDUSTRY

II.   THE PHYSICAL ENVIRONMENT

    A. Green products as a response to environmental problems

    B. Sustainability—A basis for strategy

III.   THE POLITICAL/LEGAL ENVIRONMENT

    A. Government regulation

    B. Government deregulation

IV.   THE TECHNOLOGICAL ENVIRONMENT

    A. Trends in biology

    B. Trends in electronics/telecommunications

V.   THE DEMOGRAPHIC ENVIRONMENT

    A. World Population Explosion

    B. U. S. Demographics

       1. Family structure

       2. Aging

       3. Geographical distribution

       4. Ethnic composition

VI.   THE ECONOMIC ENVIRONMENT

    A. The rich versus the poor nations

    B. International trade

VII. THE SOCIOCULTURAL ENVIRONMENT

    A. The evolution of individual values

    B. The evolution of family structure

VIII. THE COMPETITIVE ENVIRONMENT

    A. Globalization of business

    B. Impact of technology on innovation

C. Changing channels of distribution

D. New business alignment from regulation/deregulation

E. Reactions of business to values/attitudes/and lifestyles

IX. STRATEGIC ENVIRONMENTAL EVENTS

A. The impact and timing of the event

B. Response strategies

C. Ethical issues and the environment

X. SUMMARY

ANSWERS TO DISCUSSION QUESTIONS

1. **Drinking water pollution (contamination) has become a serious problem in many countries. What opportunities does this present for a variety of industries, both in terms of products and equipment?**

   Water contamination creates a variety of business opportunities, examples of which are sale of bottled water to households and businesses for drinking, water purification systems to businesses using water as a raw material, and water purification systems to municipalities. The above uses would require a variety of containers, chemicals, and machinery.

2. **Over the last decade or so, more and more countries have deregulated an increasing number of industries, including those involving telephone and telegraph. How did deregulation affect the structure of such an industry? How was the role of marketing affected in this industry? What elements of the marketing mix have become more or less important as a result of this deregulation?**

   Deregulation typically makes an industry more competitive with a reduction in the number of firms. At the outset, emphasis is placed on improved pricing practices, cost reductions, product/service differentiation including new product development, and increased emphasis on customer satisfaction. A few years later, strategies center on pricing, strategic alliances, and the development of market power. All of the marketing mix elements are affected by deregulation—product, place (distribution), price, and promotion (advertising, personal selling promotion, and publicity).

3. **Experts of a high-technology research institute predict that lightweight ceramics able to tolerate extremely high temperatures will become increasingly available at lower prices over the next decade. What industries will be affected by such a development? How?**

   A variety of industries would be affected by the development of a lightweight ceramic able to withstand extremely high temperatures including those concerned in whole or part with automobiles, trucks, airplanes, missiles, and computers.

26

4. **How did the decline in the yen's value relative to the U.S. dollar during the late 1980s affect the Japanese auto companies' competitive strategies in the U.S. market? How did they adjust their marketing programs in response to the decline?**

A predominant strategic concern of many Japanese companies is dominance in market share. A market-share-oriented strategy implies relatively low levels of prices, so that the company can gain (and hold) the volume necessary to establish lower costs. This orientation helps explain the response of Japanese companies to changes in the value of the yen vis-à-vis the dollar. For example, because of the appreciation of the yen against the dollar in the fall of the 1988, Japanese car manufacturers should have increased the retail price of their $10,000 car to $16,000 just to "stay even." However, the Japanese did not increase their car costs this amount, because of fears that they would lose market share.

5. **The president of a large manufacturer of household appliances, such as washing machines, dryers, and dishwashers, has asked you to develop a system for monitoring and evaluating the likely impact of major environmental trends. Briefly describe the major components you would include in such a strategic environmental issues management system. What major activities would be involved in the operation of such a system?**

Environmental Management Process	*Activities*
Environmental scanning	Monitor: demographic trends, changes in social values, economic trends, political/legal issues, ecological issues, etc.
Key issue identification	Isolate key issues likely to have a marketing impact.
Impact evaluation	Assess the impact of key issues.
Formulation of response strategy	Work with senior management to formulate strategies to deal with environmental changes.

6. As product manager for a large international petroleum company, you are responsible for the marketing of the firm's line of lube oil brands. You have become increasingly concerned about the long-term effect on the sales of your products of synthetic lube oils which have been dropping in price so that they are now only about 50 percent more expensive than your highest-quality brand. Up to the present they have been used almost exclusively by expensive high-speed sports cars such as Ferrari. You have given your assistant the task of evaluating the relative strengths and weaknesses of this new entrant, and estimating what marketing strategy the manufacturers of such products will employ. What information would you attempt to obtain? From what sources?

At a minimum, the following kinds of information should be collected.

A. The resources of the firms now producing these synthetic oils including those of the parent company if one is present.

B. The cost structure of these companies—especially with respect to variable versus fixed. The question of what effects scale and learning will have on costs, needs to be answered.

C. The intentions of these companies in terms of competing against lube oil at some point in the future. What is that date?

D. How these firms will compete.

1. Superior product? In what ways? Guarantees?

2. Price? Longer longevity?

3. Distribution—via major companies, wholesalers, direct to retailers, or some combination?

4. Advertising—what appeals?

SUPPLEMENTARY REFERENCES:

See Footnotes 15, 17, 22, 31

TRANSPARENCIES

Chapter exhibits for which transparency masters prepared: 5, 6, 7

CHAPTER 5
MARKETING INFORMATION

I.   THE MARKETING INFORMATION REVOLUTION

II. STANDARDIZED/COMMERCIALIZED MARKETING SYSTEMS

    A. A.C. Nielsen

    B. Geodemographic data

III. INTERNAL MARKETING DATA BASES

    A. Direct incentive programs

    B. Affinity clubs

    C. Lost customer programs

IV. THE FUTURE OF MARKETING INFORMATION SYSTEMS

V.   MARKETING RESEARCH

    A. Problem formulation

    B. Determining information needs and data sources

       1. Data sources

       2. International differences in information services

    C. Research design

       1. Exploratory research

       2. Conclusive research

    D. Sample design and size

    E. Data collection

       1. Questioning

       2. Observation

       3. Methods of questioning

    F. Tabulation and analysis

VI. COMPETITOR ANALYSIS

    A. Characteristics of the competitor

    B. Competitor's objectives

C. Strategy of the competitor

D. Evaluating success of the competitor

E. Competitor's strengths and weaknesses

F. Competitor's future behavior

VII. OBTAINING INFORMATION ABOUT COMPETITORS—DATA CONFIDENTIALITY

VIII. CUSTOMER SATISFACTION STUDIES

A. Expectation measures

B. Performance measures

IX. MARKET POTENTIAL MEASURES

A. Industry sales

B. Corollary data

1. Single-factor index

2. Multiple-factor indexes

X. MARKETING DECISION SUPPORT SYSTEMS (MDSSs)

A. How MDSS works

B. The future of MDSSs

XI. ETHICAL ISSUES IN MARKETING INFORMATION SYSTEMS AND MARKETING RESEARCH

XII. SUMMARY

ANSWERS TO DISCUSSION QUESTIONS

1. **Point of sales (POS) data such as that provided by the A.C. Nielsen Company typically includes continuous sales (tracking) information on a wide variety of products and brands sold by an array of retailers. What are the major reasons why retailers use such data? How do manufacturers use these data?**

   Retailers use POS data primarily to design programs, determine product assortments, decide amount of shelf space to allot to various items and brands, monitor the sales of new products, and measure the results of in-store promotions. Manufacturers of consumer goods use point of sale data primarily for developing strategic marketing programs, tracking new products, evaluating consumer and trade promotions, evaluating the sales force, and deciding on changes in the company's price strategies.

2. **POS data can be augmented by using demographics and purchasing-behavior information. In what ways can such augmented data be used by retailers and manufacturers?**

   Augmented POS data can be used by retailers to better understand their target markets, develop their advertising programs, and better understand the nature and scope of their competitors. Manufacturers can use such augmented data to undertake such basic analysis as those relating to products (which items to abandon), order size, distribution, and performance of individual adopters.

3. **How can a manufacturer of industrial equipment that sells direct to its customers use internally generated POS data to improve its marketing efficiency?**

   Internally generated POS can be used by a manufacturer as the basis for direct marketing and prospecting programs. It can also be used as a way of segmenting a seller's market and developing different marketing programs accordingly.

4. **A large international rental-car company decides to develop a retention program that would provide incentives for its heavy users to continue their loyalty to the company. You, as a consultant, are asked to design a retention program that will accomplish this purpose.**

   The object of a retention program of a car rental company should be to offer a direct incentive to customers for heavy usage which will encourage repeat business. Probably the most successful type of program would be similar to the airlines' frequent flyer programs—indeed, one can use them by transferring rental car revenues into mileage awards with a given airline. In a similar fashion, the rental car firm could set up its own program and award points which could be transferred into credit dollars to be used to rent the company's cars. The company could also identify its heavy users by geographical location or season of the year, and then use direct mail offer discount or trade-up coupons which are good for use during a restricted time period on certain types of company cars. The value of the discounted coupon would depend on the extent of usage.

31

5. **Before putting your recommended retention program in operation, the company asks you to prepare a marketing research project that will test the viability of your proposal.**

The program could be tested by drawing a sample of company users for the prior year and making them a special offer via a discount coupon good for a limited time period. To validate the coupon, the recipients would have to join the company's frequent mileage club, whereby they could receive credit for the points earned by using the rental car company's cars. The effectiveness of the intended program would be determined largely by the difference between the usage generated by members of the sample for the previous 12 months and the following 12 months. Also, a tabulation should be made of new customers (those who had not patronized the company during the prior 12 months).

6. **A local theater company wants to know whether current season ticket holders would prefer more comedies or more serious dramas next season. Because program decisions must be made soon, the information must be collected quickly. But the research budget is limited. Which survey questioning method (i.e., mail, phone, personal interviews) would you recommend using to collect the information? What limitations might that method impose on the study?**

This problem lends itself to a telephone survey, because this method is quick and low-cost. Further, unlike personal interviews in the mail, the method can be based on a probability sample—so the results can be examined for statistical reliability. The primary limitation (compared to other methods) is that visual materials cannot be readily displayed in a telephone survey (this could only be done with technology in place by mailing out visual materials and calling in conjunction with them). Also, some interpersonal feedback that depends on body language is lost in this approach. Another problem is that refusal rates are high and increasing due to an overload on consumers from a variety of companies.

7. **The household detergents division of a large household products company with worldwide distribution is planning a research study among women 21 years and over to determine their attitudes toward home laundering and the products and brands used in such activities. Studies are to be carried out in a variety of countries in the Far East, Middle East, Africa, Western Europe, Eastern Europe, and South America. What data-collection problems would you expect to experience in doing this research across a variety of countries?**

The problems which will be encountered in doing such research across a variety of countries include the difficulties associated with sample design (inadequate population data), questionnaire design, hiring/training/control over interviewers, data collection methods (phone versus personal interviewing), and actual data collecting (asking questions and recording answers). It will be difficult to compare the results across countries given the variation in the sample designs, the response rates of different groups, the caliber of the interviewers, and the meaning of key words in the questionnaire.

8. **A company making high-speed modems—devices that cover signals from one type of machine (computer) to a form compatible with another (telephone)—was concerned that its latest modem, which had just been introduced to the market in the previous month, would soon be upstaged by yet a faster device produced by a major competitor. Your marketing research company has been hired to profile data about this competitor regarding its objectives (short-term/long-term), its R&D capabilities, and the likelihood of its introducing a higher-speed modem than yours in the immediate future. You ask the research firm to present a plan for obtaining such data. Outline the major parts of your proposed plan including the data you want and how you will obtain it.**

The major parts of the proposed plan, data wanted, and method of obtaining that data are as follows:

  a. *Competitor's Characteristics*

  —data include revenues, share growth (trends), profitability, financial resources, new product trends, strength of R&D resources, and relations to parent company (if necessary).

  —sources include industry publications, industry experts, competitor's past behavior, own sales force, former executives of competitor, and analysis of educational qualification and job experience of key R&D personnel.

  b. *Company Objectives*

  —market share and revenues, product technology, history of technology successes and failures, prior response to being relegated to lower position on technology rating, and weight put behind typical product launch.

  —sources include most of those listed under competitor's characteristics plus benchmarking present products(s) to determine the feasibility of modifying them to obtain product superiority.

  c. *Competitor's Strengths and Weaknesses*

  —can be largely deduced from information cited under first two headings.

  —many of same sources already cited plus interviews from company's major accounts.

9. After accepting your proposed retention program, the car rental firm (see questions 4 and 5) asks your marketing-research firm to develop a major study designed to provide detailed information about the extent to which their customers are satisfied with the service they receive. You are expected to indicate what customer-satisfaction measures you plan to use, the information you intend to obtain, and the sample you will use (both in terms of the type of respondents and how they will be selected).

Respondents will be drawn from users of the company's service during the past 12 months. Each will be asked what their choice criteria is for selecting a rental car company (i.e., what attributes are important and the relative importance of each). They are then asked to rate the company's service versus a number of competitors. The difference in the ratings (ideal versus actual) is the gap which reveals the extent of disappointment. By getting selected demographic information as well as usage information, further breakdowns can be made.

10. Given that absolute market potential almost always exceeds actual industry sales, why do marketers bother to make potential estimates? Discuss four decisions that a marketer of industrial grinding machinery might make based on such potential estimates.

Thinking in terms of market potential expands the thinking of management. Marking is virtually the only open-ended business function, in that the upper limits are not set by the nature of the problem; understanding demand potential is a prerequisite to estimating industry sales and, hence, company sales. Production is given levels based on sales. Finance attempts to minimize the cost of capital to produce at those levels. But marketing essentially sets the levels. Thus, thinking in terms of potentials becomes a critical way of thinking for the marketer.

In this case, the industrial grinding machinery might use such potentials to (1) allocate advertising efforts among areas or product-markets; (2) determine sales quotas; (3) determine sale territories; and (4) locate sales offices, warehouses, and plants.

11. To more effectively allocate promotion expenditures and sales efforts, the marketing manager for a company marketing frozen food entrees would like to know the relative market potential for such products in every county in the United States. What variables would you include in a multifactor index for measuring relative potential? Explain your rationale for including each variable. Where might you find up-to-date information about each of the variables in your index?

34

Variable	Source	Rationale
Females age 25-50	Census of Population	Weight-conscious segment of the population
Discretionary	Sales & Marketing	Stouffer's product is targeted at a relatively high-price, high-quality segment
Working females	Census of Population	Time-conscious consumers, oriented toward quick preparation

12. **A small snowmobile manufacturer wants to add two new dealerships in a northern region of a midwestern state. Given the following information about the counties in the region, where would you recommend locating the two new dealerships?**

County	Population (000)	Total sales ($)	County sales ($)
A	161.3	$1,400.5	$93.1
B	13.4	70.0	19.0
C	72.0	227.5	36.0
D	361.7	1,417.5	180.5
E	16.2	875.0	418.0
F	56.2	1,155.0	77.5
Total:			
County	680.8	$5,144.5	$824.1
State	3,583.4	$14,000	$1,600.0

County	% State Pop (1)	% State Sales (2)	% Co. Sales (3)	Ind. Penetra. 4 = (211)	Company Penetra. 5 = (311)	Opportunity Index 6 = (415)
A	4.50	10.00	5.82	2.22	1.29	1.72
B	0.37	00.50	1.19	1.35	3.22	0.42
C	2.00	01.63	2.25	0.80	1.13	0.73
D	10.09	10.13	11.28	1.00	1.12	0.89
E	0.45	0.63	26.13	1.40	58.07	0.02
F	1.57	0.83	4.84	0.53	3.08	0.17

Based on these simple statistics, county A would appear to have the greatest potential. Note that this is based on historical sales, and does not measure the latent market (i.e., people who haven't bought yet but might).

13. What are the dangers involved in using salesforce estimates to forecast a product's future sales? Under which conditions are such estimates most likely to be accurate and useful?

The salesforce estimate may have an upward or downward bias. A downward bias is particularly likely if the sales forecast is tied to quota goals. Further, salespeople are unlikely to know about other marketing efforts (such as planned advertising campaigns) that would affect future sales. However, salesforce estimates are particularly useful for short-term forecasts during especially volatile market.

SUPPLEMENTARY REFERENCES:

See Footnotes 1, 2, 3, 9, 10, 18

TRANSPARENCIES:

Chapter exhibits for which transparency masters prepared: 4

CHAPTER 6
INDUSTRY DYNAMICS AND STRATEGIC CHANGE

C. Major forces determining industry competition

    1. Present competitors

    2. Threat of new entrants

    3. Bargaining strengths of suppliers

    4. Bargaining strengths of buyers

    5. Threat of substitute products

D. Changing competition and industry evolution

VIII. SUMMARY

ANSWERS TO DISCUSSION QUESTIONS

1. **The rewards for being one of the first firms to develop a line of digital TV sets are thought to be substantial—despite the large investment required. Why is it that firms will benefit from being among the first to take advantage of such an environmental opportunity? What risks are involved?**

   Firms benefit from being among the first to take advantage of an environmental opportunity by becoming the standard against which later entrants are compared. Also, the leader has the first choice of market segments and can appropriate the better middlemen as well as the major promotion appeals. In addition, the leader can derive a substantial advantage through scale effects and its learning curve. Being first is not, however, without its risks, the biggest ones of which have to do with misjudging the size of the market, the extent to which the product is sufficiently better than alternatives, the positioning of the product, and whether short-term changes in the relevant technology will strongly benefit followers.

2. **The value of any product life-cycle analysis depends to a great extent upon how the product is defined and what market level is used for defining the target market. Using ready-to-eat cereals as your example, what product level would you use, coupled with what market level?**

   For the purpose of a product life-cycle analysis for ready-to-eat cereals, the product should be defined in terms of subtypes such as corn flakes, raisin bran, and shredded wheat. Much depends here on how the industry defines those products. For example, the trade press often reports certain marketing data by such types as presweetened. The market level choice would depend on who was using the data and for what purposes. Sales management would want the market level to coincide with their sales districts—possibly even their sales territories while advertising managers would want the market choice to center on certain demographics and product usage (heavy versus light users).

3. **What is the value of using the life cycle concept? What are the concept's limitations?**

   The product life-cycle model provides a conceptual framework which signals the occurrence of opportunities and threats in the marketplace and the investment requirements for success. It also indicates how the firm's strategy and marketing programs must change as the product moves through the various life-cycle stages. The major weakness of the concept lies in its normative approach to prescribing strategies based on assumptions about the characteristics of each stage. More specifically, it fails to take into account the major forces driving the life cycle—the evolution of consumer preferences, technology, and competition.

4. **Although Levi's basic blue jeans experienced a period of increased popularity and sales growth a few years ago, the product's life-cycle curve has undergone several "cycle-recycle" phases throughout its history. Which factors might account for this life-cycle pattern?**

Essentially, jeans are a high-involvement, highly differentiated product class. As such, the product is prone to a sort of "social variety seeking." They continue to grow in sales over time, and then because they have been socially visible for a prolonged period, decline in popularity (i.e., "go out of fashion").

5. **Suppose you are the product manager for a new aseptic packaging material which preserves milk and other dairy products without refrigeration. The product is in the introductory stage of its life cycle. What are the implications of this position in the decisions you must make about each of the 4 Ps when designing a strategic marketing program for this product? What (and if) this product reaches the growth stage, what changes will you have to make in your marketing plan, including its objectives?**

Aseptic packages are in the introductory stage of their life cycle, where there are few segments and a small number of competitors. The essential marketing objective is primary demand stimulation (building up a market for the product) rather than secondary demand stimulation (building up a market for the brand). The company should seek quality improvement, keep its product line narrow, price to penetrate the market, use its own sales force, and seek publicity in trade journals. As the market grows, the company should seek to build market share, continue to make quality improvements, widen its product line, reduce its price, and build a strong sales service organization.

6. **The U.S. market for color TVs is mature and has experienced relatively little growth in recent years. If you were the marketing manager for Sony color TVs, what marketing strategy would you recommend?**

The standard advice for mature product markets is to concentrate on product features (e.g., color quality, resolution), hold the length of the product line, maintain or reduce prices, continue intensive distribution, and maintain or gradually decrease marketing communications efforts.

An optional strategy might be to attempt to identify a growth niche within the color TV market (e.g., wide screen TVs, component systems) and follow a growth strategy within that niche. Thus, if wide screen TVs are growing substantially (even though the overall color TV market is not), within that niche it might be appropriate to offer continued quality improvements, a broad line, reduced prices, intensive distribution, and a high level of marketing communications (mass media) efforts.

Another option might be to attempt a new product introduction, such as high-resolution TV.

7. Suppose you are the product manager responsible for General Electric's line of trash compactors. After more than ten years, the product has yet to gain acceptance by many consumers. Using the diffusion of innovations theory discussed in the text, explain why trash compactors have achieved such poor market penetration. What does this imply concerning the shape of the rest of the trash compactor's life-cycle curve?

Among the factors that affect the rate of adoption are risk, simplicity, availability for trail, and ease with which the core concept can be communicated. The trash compactor replaces the trash can, and yet is higher in (financial) risk, is somewhat more complex to operate, and typically is not displayed in a situation where trial is convenient. The core concept is somewhat difficult to communicate; i.e., the convenience and time savings of reducing the frequency of trash-to-garbage can trips.

Because it replaces one product with another, substantially different product, it is likely to gain slow acceptance. The most important communications mode is likely to be word of mouth, as people see trash compactors in use in daily life, in homes of opinion leaders. Yet this effect is likely to be subdued by the fact that this is not a visible, prestigious item. Thus, the product life cycle is likely to be slow growth, stable maturity, slow decline.

SUPPLEMENTARY REFERENCES:

See Footnotes 9, 14, 15, 16, 19, 23

TRANSPARENCIES:

Chapter exhibits for which transparency masters prepared: 1, 2, 3, 4, 7, 10

CHAPTER 7
MARKET SEGMENTATION AND MARKET TARGETING

I. SEGMENTING THE SPORTS APPAREL MARKET

II. SEGMENTATION TARGETING AND POSITIONING

III. RATIONALE FOR MARKET SEGMENTATION

    A. Growing importance of segmentation

    B. Benefits of segmentation

IV. THE SEGMENTATION PROCESS

V. IDENTIFICATION OF MARKET SEGMENTS

    A. Physical descriptors

    B. General behavioral descriptors

        1. Lifestyle

        2. Social class

        3. Interest

        4. Industrial or firm behavioral descriptors

    C. Product-related behavioral descriptors

    D. Customer needs

VI. GLOBAL MARKET SEGMENTATION

VII. SERVICE SEGMENTATION

VIII. MARKET ATTRACTIVENESS

    A. Analyzing and Prioritizing Potential Target Markets

    B. Steps Used to Develop Market Attractiveness/Business Position Matrix for Analyzing Current and Potential Target Markets

        1. Select market attractiveness and business strength factors

        2. Weigh each attractiveness and business strength factor

        3. Rate each segment as to its market attractiveness and company strengths

        4. Project future position of a market

        5. Evaluate consequences for choosing target markets and allocating resources

ANSWERS TO DISCUSSION QUESTIONS

1. **Extensive market segmentation is a relatively recent phenomenon. Until about the middle of this century many firms offered a single basic product aimed at the entire mass market (such as Coca-Cola or Levi jeans). But in recent years many firms—including industrial goods manufacturers and services producers as well as consumer products companies—have begun segmenting their markets and developing different products and marketing programs targeted at different segments. Which environmental changes have helped spark this increased interest in market segmentation? Which advantages or benefits can a firm gain from properly segmenting its market?**

   Environmental changes that have increased interest in market segmentation include: (1) slowing of population growth and maturing of product markets (which increase competition among firms within the industry and markets); (2) social and economic forces that have increased the demand for product variety; and (3) segmenting of services by institutions serving consumers (in effect, derived segmentation).

   Advantages or benefits to segmentation include the fact that segmentation: (1) reflects the realities of products and marketing programs that are most effective for reaching homogenous groups of customers; (2) can identify opportunities for new-product development; (3) can improve the strategic allocation of marketing resources.

2. **Is market segmentation always a good idea? Under which conditions, if any, might segmentation be unnecessary or unwise?**

   The ultimate segment is one customer in one usage situation. Each potential customer in an identifiable usage situation represents a segment, and the number of segments that will respond to differences in the marketing mix (such as slight variations in product, price, distribution, promotion) is equal to the population times the number of usage situations applicable to each member.

   Clearly, it is not feasible for Campbell to make a different soup with just the right blend of flavors, with just the right advertising appeal, at just the right price, just where you want it. So Campbell makes soups that appeal to distinct groups of people (like you), perhaps down to regions of the country (like spicy varieties for the Southwest).

   In short, segmentation becomes unnecessary or unwise if the segment is too small (to be profitable), if further bases of segmentation are difficult to measure (e.g., soup for hypochondriacs), if these segments are hard to reach (again, soup for hypochondriacs), or if the difference in the new subsegment's response to a new marketing mix is not significantly different from that of the more broadly defined segments.

3. Which variable or descriptors might be most appropriate for segmenting the market for the following consumer products and services? Explain your reasoning.

   a. **Lawn mowers**

   b. **Frozen entrées or dinners**

   c. **Breakfast cereals**

   d. **Financial services**

Product	Segment Descriptors
Lawn mower	Family life cycle (home size may vary)
	Age, sex (requirements for self-propelled, starting features)
	Income (receptivity to expense)
Frozen dinner/entrée	Psychographics (weight consciousness)
	Income (price elasticity)
Breakfast cereal	Age
Financial services	Family life cycle (affects investment needs)

4. Which variable or descriptors might be most appropriate for segmenting the markets for the following industrial goods and services? Explain your reasoning.

   a. **Photocopiers**

   b. **Floor sweepers**

   c. **Truck leasing**

Product	Segment Descriptors
Photocopiers	Purchasing structure (sell to HQ or unit?)
	Company size (photocopy needs may vary)
	Hierarchical position (perhaps mid- to low-)
Floor sweepers	Company size (needs may vary)
Truck leasing	Purchasing structure (lease to HQ or unit?)
	Company size (needs may vary)
	Hierarchical position (perhaps mid- to high-)

5. A camera manufacturer has hired you as a consultant to identify major *benefit segments* in the camera market. Which major benefit segments do you think might exist in this market, without actually conducting consumer research? What other information would you want to collect about the potential customers in each segment to provide a useful basis for designing camera models and marketing programs that appeal to each segment?

Industrial Markets
Providing ability to do primary work.
(e.g., professional photographer)

Providing ability to do secondary work.
(e.g., Realtor)

Consumer Markets
Providing personal/family momentos.

Providing social interaction
(as with instant films).
Providing hobby, recreation.

Information Needed
Professional journals read.
Variety of equipment utilized.
Usage situations.

Usage situations.

Skill levels.
Price elasticity.

Price elasticity.

Price elasticity.
Usage situations.

6. How would you know whether the segmentation variables you identified in the above question actually define effective and useful segments of customers? What criteria would you use to evaluate the effectiveness of your segmentation scheme?

Criteria required for effective market segmentation include:

(a) Adequate size (i.e., Is it big enough to be profitable to prepare a unique marketing mix for?);

(b) Measurability (i.e., Can the Descriptor be measured?);

(c) Accessibility (i.e., Can the segment be reached by some medium?); and

(d) Differential response (i.e., Does the segment respond differently than other segments to a unique marketing mix?).

7. **You are the marketing manager for a medium-sized U.S. packaged food company which has decided to market its product in Europe. What segmentation scheme would you use and what limitations would it have in helping you identify your target markets?**

There are several levels of segmentation involved. First, there is segmentation by country; second, by area within the country; and third, by consumer demographics. The limitations are that this segmentation scheme fails to take into account the relative importance of various consumer groups across countries, thereby biasing the selection of countries. Further, it does not provide for any behavioral factors except those which can be inferred from demographic descriptors used.

8. **What is the difference between a *growth market* targeting strategy and a *niche* targeting strategy? What capabilities or strengths should a business have to implement a growth market targeting strategy effectively?**

A growth market strategy, as the name implies, concentrates on identifying *fast-growth* segments of the market. A niche strategy serves one or more segments, which, while perhaps not the largest, offer the firm a substantial enough number of customers to be successful. In a niche strategy there is no requirement on the growth of a particular niche.

A growth market targeting strategy often is best suited to smaller firms who wish to avoid direct confrontation with larger firms. This strategy requires strong R&D and marketing capabilities to identify and develop products. It also requires the necessary financial resources to finance rapid growth.

9. **Which market targeting strategy was Honda pursuing when it first entered the U.S. market with its low-priced Civic automobile? How has their strategy changed over the years?**

Honda followed a growth market strategy when it first entered the U.S. car market. They believed correctly, that small, inexpensive automobiles would become an important market in the auto industry. Since the introduction of the Civic, Honda has developed cars for other target markets (such as the Prelude, which is more sporty, and Accord, which is larger and more upscale than the Civic).

10. **In developing a targeting matrix, what dangers are incurred? How can these dangers be minimized?**

The major drawback is that the factors involved as well as their ratings are subjective in nature and yet give the impression of being precise. A further weakness is that the factors used may not be independent of each and hence are improperly weighted in the scoring.

Ways of minimizing the subjectivity cited above is to generate as much objective data about each of the market attractiveness sectors as well as the competitive position factors. A second way is to bring the managers involved together after they have completed their ratings to discuss/debate their differences.

SUPPLEMENTARY REFERENCES:

See Footnotes 3, 5, 6, 12, 15, 23 25

TRANSPARENCIES:

Chapter exhibits for which transparency masters prepared: 1, 4, 7, 8, 9, 10, 11

CHAPTER 8
POSITIONING DECISIONS

I.   REPOSITIONING FRENCH WINE

II. REQUIREMENTS FOR SUCCESSFUL POSITIONING

III. PHYSICAL VERSUS PERCEPTUAL PRODUCT POSITIONING

   A. Limitations of physical positioning

   B. Perceptual product positioning

   C. Dimensions on which consumers perceive competitive offerings

IV. THE POSITIONING PROCESS

   A. Identify a relevant set of competitive products (step 1)

   B. Identify determinant attributes (step 2)

   C. Determine consumers' perceptions (step 3)

   D. Analyze the intensity of a product's current position (step 4)

      1. Marketing opportunities to gain positioning intensity

      2. Constraints imposed by an intense position

   E. Analyze the product's current position (step 5)

   F. Determine consumers' preferred combination of attributes (step 6)

   G. Define market positioning and market segmentation (step 7)

H. Select positioning strategies

    1. Sales potential of market positions (step 8)

    2. Market positioning strategies

       —Monosegment positioning

       —Multisegment positioning

       —Standby positioning

       —Imitative positioning

       —Anticipatory positioning

       —Adaptive positioning

       —Defensive positioning

    3. Positioning of services

V. SUMMARY

ANSWERS TO DISCUSSION QUESTIONS

1. **What are the major differences between physical and perceptual product positioning? Under what conditions would a firm be satisfied with simply a physical position exercise? What kinds of firms would practice this kind of positioning? What dangers are involved?**

The major differences between physical and perceptual product positioning is that the former is based on some set of objective physical characteristics. Such positioning can provide useful information, particularly in the early stages of designing new product offerings—especially so with industrial goods. It also helps marketing in interfacing with R&D. But a comparison of alternative offerings based only on the physical dimensions of alternative offerings does not provide a complete picture of relative positions since positioning ultimately takes place in the consumers' minds—i.e., it depends on how the product/brand is perceived. The evaluation of many products is subjective since it is determined by factors other than physical properties. Undertaking a perceptual product positioning is therefore critical.

2. **What exactly does perceptual positioning accomplish for a consumer goods firm? For an industrial goods firm?**

Since many consumer goods brands are similar in their physical characteristics, it is important to undertake a perceptual product positioning study to determine if consumers perceive them as being similar or being different because of different histories, names, and consumer attitudes. It is also important to note how competing brands differ, not only from each other but against the consumer's ideal brand. For industrial groups a perceptual positioning study will reveal how various customer groups perceive a given product on the basis of both its physical and nonphysical characteristics. In some cases the latter can be extremely important (e.g., service dimensions).

3. **What determines the *intensity* of a product's perceived position in the marketplace? What might be done to increase the intensity of the position of a brand that currently holds a relatively small market share, such as Saab in the automobile market or Clinique in the cosmetics market?**

Perhaps most important, the positioning intensity of a brand depends on how strongly customers associate it with one or more determinant attributes when deciding which to buy. In addition, another factor is how strongly customers associate the brand with the product category.

Establish an intense position by focusing on one or two key determinant attributes, as P&G did with Crest when it focused on decay prevention and received the endorsement of the American Dental Association. A better option for a firm holding a small market share, however, may be to concentrate on an attribute not strongly associated with the dominant brand, and to position itself as a feasible substitute for bigger brands under certain situations, or for targeting a peripheral segment of the market.

4. **What is meant by *determinant attribute* for a given product? Explain why the identification of such attributes is so important. What would be an example of a determinant attribute for four-wheel-drive (off-road) vehicles?**

Consumers typically use a relatively small number of attributes to evaluate products and brands. Consumers first consider only those attributes they are aware of, but the importance attached to those often varies. Even an important attribute may not be a strong influence on a consumer's preference if the alternative brands are perceived as being about equal on that dimension. A determinant attribute is one which plays a major role in helping consumers differentiate among the alternatives and determine which brand they prefer. In the case of Ford's Explorer the ability of the driver to switch from two-wheel to four-wheel drive by simply pressing a button (even when driving) was a determinant attribute since Jeep Cherokee required drivers to use a lever to make the change.

5. **Exhibit 8.7 is a perceptual map of women's clothing retailers in Washington, DC which shows the ideal points of a given segment of consumers. What is an *ideal point* and how is it determined? How can it be used in relation to the development of a strategic marketing plan?**

To measure customer preferences requires that respondents rate their ideal product or brand within a product category and use this as the basis for rating existing products. The results will show how the various brands are positioned versus the ideal. These ideal points can be clustered for a given market segment to determine its preferences. By comparing how (and why) the competing brands differ from one another based on their distances from one another and the cluster of ideal points, a firm can decide whether a new product concept is viable or what needs to be done to reposition an existing brand which will result in greater revenues.

6. **For a high-quality women's clothing retailer like Nordstrom, what would be the best market position strategy to adopt? Why?**

Nordstrom already has an enviable position in terms of value and fashion ability. It could improve this position slightly by moving closer to segment 4.

7. **In terms of positioning strategy, what is the rationale for the fact that Nabisco offers many different brands within the cracker category, each of which is perceived as being only slightly different from the others? What are the advantages and limitations of such a strategy?**

Nabisco may wish to preempt a strong move by the competition by introducing a second, similar brand positioned to appeal to the same market segment.

Advantages—it is better in the long run for a firm to compete with itself than to lose customers to other firms.

Disadvantages—cannibalizes the market of the established brand, results in higher investments, lower economies of scale.

SUPPLEMENTARY REFERENCES:

See Footnotes 2, 4, 7, 8, 18

TRANSPARENCIES:

Chapter exhibits for which transparency masters prepared: 2, 3, 4, 5, 6, 7, 8, 9, 10

CHAPTER 9
MARKETING STRATEGIES FOR NEW MARKET ENTRIES

I. ILLINOIS TOOL WORKS—NEW NUTS & BOLTS TO FILL MANY NICHES

II. SOME ISSUES CONCERNING NEW MARKET ENTRY STRATEGIES

III. HOW NEW IS "NEW"?

IV. OBJECTIVES OF NEW PRODUCT AND MARKET DEVELOPMENT

V. MARKET ENTRY STRATEGIES: PIONEERS VERSUS FOLLOWERS

    A. Pioneer Strategy

    B. Not All Pioneers Capitalize on Their Potential Advantages

    C. Follower Strategy

    D. Determinants of Success for Pioneers and Followers

VI. STRATEGIC MARKETING PROGRAMS FOR POINEERS

    A. Mass-Market Penetration

    B. Niche Penetration Strategy

    C. Skimming and Early Withdrawal

    D. Objectives of Alternative Pioneer Strategies

    E. Marketing Program Components for a Mass-Market Penetration Strategy

        1. Increasing customers' awareness and willingness to buy

        2. Increasing customers' ability to buy

        3. Additional considerations for pioneering global markets

    F. Marketing Program Components for a Niche Penetration Strategy

    G. Marketing Program Components for a Skimming Strategy

VII. SUMMARY

ANSWERS TO DISCUSSION QUESTIONS

1. **Minnetonka, Inc. was a relatively small firm that pioneered the development of a number of consumer health and beauty products—such as Softsoap and Check-Up plaque fighting toothpaste—over recent years. What *potential advantages* did being the pioneer in new product markets provide a firm like Minnetonka in an industry dominated by giants such as Procter & Gamble and Colgate-Palmolive? What strategic marketing activities should Minnetonka have pursued in order to maximize its chances at being able to gain and maintain a leading share position in those new markets?**

The *potential* advantages associated with being a new product pioneer include:

1. First choice of target market segments and positions;

2. The opportunity to define the competitive "rules of the game";

3. Possible distribution advantages;

4. The opportunity to gain economies of scale and experience;

5. High switching costs for early adopters;

6. Possible opportunity to preempt scarce resources and suppliers.

The evidence suggests that a pioneer is most likely to build upon and benefit from these potential sources of first-mover advantage when it does one or more of the following things: (1) enters the market at—or quickly achieves—a large scale, (2) rapidly extends its product line, (3) achieves and maintains high product quality, and (4) supports its entry with heavy promotional expenditures. Since Minnetonka could not hope to match P&G's large-scale production and distribution capabilities or its promotional resources, a focus on high product quality and the rapid introduction of line extensions aimed at peripheral market segments should have been key elements of the firm's competitive strategy.

2. Unfortunately, Minnetonka, Inc. was one of those pioneers that proved unable to sustain its early lead in the new markets it entered. The firm's Check-Up toothpaste, for example, quickly lost ground to follower P&G's plaque fighting Crest. What strategic factors might account for Procter & Gamble's success at capturing strong market shares as a follower in markets pioneered by Minnetonka?

Followers can overcome a pioneer's advantage by:

1. Entering the market at a larger scale—or with more resources—than the pioneer;

2. Leapfrogging the pioneer by developing superior technology, product quality, and/or service;

3. Observing and correcting the pioneer's mistakes.

Even though Minnetonka did not make any major marketing blunders and its major competitors introduced largely "me-too" products and marketing programs, those competitors had such well-established brand names (e.g., Crest) and sufficiently superior production capacities, marketing and promotional resources, and distribution strengths, that they were quickly able to "out-muscle" Minnetonka in the plaque-fighting toothpaste market and overcome the firm's early market share lead.

3. **With the exception of certain "core businesses"—such as adhesives and information storage technology—the 3M Company has often followed a strategy of withdrawing from markets in which it was the pioneer after other competitors enter and profit margins start to decline. It typically does this by licensing products to other firms. Under what kinds of market and competitive situations is such a withdrawal strategy most appropriate? What kinds of products do you think 3M is most likely to license to other firms?**

A "skimming/early withdrawal" strategy tends to be most appropriate when one or more of the following conditions are likely to hold in the market:

1. Total demand is likely to be limited;

2. Many of the largest potential customers are likely to quickly adopt the new product and be relatively insensitive to price;

3. Many potential competitors exist and have the capabilities necessary to enter and effectively compete for a share of the market.

3M is most likely to license a product to other firms when:

1. The product's technology cannot be effectively protected for very long;

2. The resources necessary to produce the product are commonly available;

3. The product is not directly related to one of the firm's "core" technologies;

4. 3M has no unique marketing or sales capabilities with which to sustain a competitive advantage.

4. **In order for 3M to profitably implement a strategy of "skimming and early withdrawal" in a particular new product-market, what specific marketing objectives should they pursue in that market? What marketing actions would be appropriate for achieving those objectives?**

The major objective should be to maximize ROI in the short term. Therefore, the marketing objective should be to win as many early adopters as possible while holding investment to a minimum.

Marketing actions consistent with these objectives include:

1. A "skimming" price policy based on value received by early adopters;

2. Limited advertising and promotional programs tightly focused on the segment(s) most likely to be early adopters and to attach high value to the new product;

3. Extensive personal selling efforts focused on the above segment(s);

4. Programs and services (e.g., installation, financing, user-training, etc.) aimed at increasing potential early adopters' ability and willingness to buy.

5. **Sun Microsystems is a relatively small firm by computer industry standards. It has been very successful at capturing a substantial—and profitable—share of the market for specialized mid-sized computer systems used for computer-assisted design and engineering applications. Given the characteristics of the computer industry and its environment, do you think Sun's niche penetration strategy continues to be appropriate? Why or why not?**

Sun's strategy is appropriate for a relatively small firm that continues to face much larger competitors. By focusing on a relatively narrow—but rapidly growing—niche, Sun has been able to grow with its market without over-running its limited resources or directly confronting its larger competitors. While bigger firms such as IBM and H-P are now focusing on Sun's market, the firm continues to benefit from its accumulated knowledge and experience—and its close contacts and relationships with major customers—in that market.

SUPPLEMENTARY REFERENCES:

See Footnotes 3, 4, 5, 7, 8

TRANSPARENCIES:

Chapter exhibits for which transparency masters prepared: 1, 2, 3, 4, 5, 6, 8, 9

CHAPTER 10
STRATEGIES FOR GROWTH MARKETS

I. J&J's VISTAKON—A CHALLENGER CAPTURES THE LEADING SHARE OF THE CONTACT LENS MARKET

II. STRATEGIC ISSUES IN GROWTH MARKETS

III. OPPORTUNITIES AND RISKS IN GROWTH MARKETS

    A. Gaining share is easier

    B. Share gains are worth more

    C. Price competition is likely to be less intense

    D. Early entry is necessary to maintain technical expertise

IV. GROWTH-MARKET STRATEGIES FOR MARKET LEADERS

    A. Marketing objectives for share leaders

    B. Marketing actions and strategies to achieve share-maintenance objectives

    C. Fortress, or position defense, strategy

        1. Actions to improve customer satisfaction and loyalty

        2. Actions to encourage and simplify repeat purchasing

        3. Building long-term relationships with customers

        4. The importance of trust

        5. Conditions favoring trust and commitment

    D. Flanker strategy

    E. Confrontation strategy

    F. Market expansion or mobile strategy

    G. Contraction or strategic withdrawal

V. SHARE GROWTH STRATEGIES FOR FOLLOWERS

    A. Marketing objectives for followers

    B. Marketing actions and strategies to achieve share growth

    C. Deciding whom to attack

    D. Frontal attack strategy

ANSWERS TO DISCUSSION QUESTIONS

1. **During the 1980s, Stouffer's Foods held a commanding share of the growing market for low calorie frozen entrées with its Lean Cuisine product line. In order to maintain its lead as the market continued to grow, what strategic objectives did or should Stouffer's have focused on and why? What specific marketing actions would you have recommended for accomplishing Stouffer's objectives? Be specific with regard to each of "4 Ps" in the firm's marketing program.**

   As the share leader, Stouffer's should focus on retaining current customers by (1) maintaining and improving the satisfaction and loyalty, (2) encouraging and simplifying repeat purchases, and (3) reducing the attractiveness of switching to one of the newer entrants into the market. Because the market continued to grow, Stouffer's should have also stimulated selective demand among later adopters, probably by trying to maintain a differentiated position from its many followers on the basis of product quality. Possible marketing actions include:

   - Product
     - —strengthen quality control procedures
     - —product & process improvements to maintain quality differentiation
     - —line extensions to appeal to segments with different tastes
     - —expand production capacity as needed to keep up with demand

   - Price
     - —maintain premium price consistent with quality difference, but price differential may have to be reduced if competitors achieve comparable quality

   - Place
     - —line extensions to increase shelf facings
     - —trade promotions as necessary to maintain distribution in face of increased competition

   - Promotion
     - —reminder advertising targeted at current customers
     - —advertising focused on selective demand and trial for late adopters
     - —promotions to stimulate repeat purchase and loyalty among current users (e.g., in-pack coupons, multi-pack deals, etc.)
     - —promotions to stimulate trial among late adopters

2. **During the early 1990s, Conagra challenged Stouffer's Lean Cuisine with its Healthy Choice line of frozen entrées. The Healthy Choice line has managed to capture a substantial and growing share of the market. What strategy did (or could) Conagra use to achieve success against more established competitors such as Stouffer's? What marketing actions would be critical keys to the success of that strategy?**

Conagra's share building strategy has consisted of a combination of *leapfrogging* on the basis of superior product formulations and attributes (e.g., not only low calorie, but also low sodium, low fat, and more nutritious offerings), and *encirclement* by targeting various new market niches (e.g., such as desserts) and by developing line extensions into nonfrozen categories (e.g., low-fat cheeses, condiments, etc.). Competence in R&D, rapid product development processes, flexible manufacturing operations, effective advertising and consumer promotions, and a skilled salesforce (and adequate trade support) that could attain shelf space for the firm's new offerings and maintain good relations with major supermarket chains, have been crucial for the success of Healthy Choice.

3. **For decades Caterpillar, Inc. held a commanding market share lead in the growing worldwide market for bulldozers and graders used in heavy construction. It achieved its position by offering high quality equipment and excellent post-sale service at premium prices. During the mid-1980s, however, Komatsu—a Japanese manufacturer—challenged Caterpillar's leading position by somewhat lower levels of quality and service but at much lower prices (i.e., a flank attack), and by designing specialized equipment for unique market niches (i.e., an encirclement strategy). Suppose you were a top marketing executive at Caterpillar. Describe two strategies that the firm might adopt to fend off Komatsu's assault and maintain its leading share position. Which would you recommend and why?**

Possible strategies for Caterpillar include:

- Fortress defense —build on existing strengths by further improving product and service quality
- Flanker —bring out a second line with lower quality and prices to meet or beat Komatsu
- Confrontation —seek to reduce costs—possibly by cutting quality & service—to meet Komatsu's prices across the entire product line
- Market expansion —develop line extensions to meet Komatsu's offering in specialized niches

Caterpillar actually adopted a *combination* of Fortress, Market Expansion, and Confrontation strategies. The firm upgraded its product design and production processes to simultaneously maintain or improve product quality while reducing costs. It also maintained its superior customer service system. Thus, it was able to build on its competitive strengths and continue to command a price premium for superior value over

Komatsu, but lower costs enabled it to reduce the size of the price differential it had to seek. Caterpillar also developed a number of new products to appeal to specialized segments with unique needs where the firm had been especially vulnerable.

4. **How would you characterize the early strategies of the major Japanese auto makers (e.g., Toyota, Nissan and Honda) when they first entered the U.S. auto market in the 1960s and 1970s? What marketing variables do you think were critical to the ultimate success of their strategies?**

Initially, the Japanese manufacturers pursued a *flank attack*, providing cars that appealed to the price-sensitive segment of U.S. auto buyers who were interested in more inexpensive, fuel efficient, reasonably reliable cars than anything the American manufacturers were offering at the time. Low prices and good product reliability—as measured by relatively low repair rates—were critical aspects of their initial marketing strategies.

5. **If you had been the top marketing executive at General Motors during the early years of the Japanese invasion of the U.S. auto market, what strategy would you have recommended to defend GM's leading market share against this new competitive threat? Why do you think GM failed to adopt such a strategy at the time?**

The U.S. automakers probably should have been quicker to adopt a flanker defense of their own and developed line extensions—or new car lines—targeted at the growing segment of young buyers who were interested in low priced, fuel efficient, reliable cars. One major reason for their reluctance to adopt such a strategy was the fact that smaller, lower priced cars provided much lower margins than existing large and mid-size lines, and they were afraid to "cannibalize" the market for those higher margin autos. Also, they underestimated the magnitude of the shift in buyer preferences resulting from the large increase in young baby-boom buyers, the rapid increase in gas prices, etc. And they may have underestimated the magnitude of the competitive threat, refusing to believe that the Japanese were capable of producing cars with sufficient quality, performance, and attractiveness to appeal to American buyers.

SUPPLEMENTARY REFERENCES

See Footnotes 1, 3, 4, 9, 11, 13, 15, 18

TRANSPARENCIES

Chapter exhibits for which transparency masters prepared: 1, 3, 4, 5, 6, 7, 8, 9, 12

CHAPTER 11
STRATEGIES FOR MATURE AND DECLINING MARKETS

I. JOHNSON CONTROLS—MAKING MONEY IN MATURE MARKETS

II. STRATEGIC ISSUES IN MATURE AND DECLINING MARKETS

    A. Issues during the transition to market maturity

    B. Issues in mature markets

    C. Issues in declining markets

III. SHAKEOUT: THE TRANSITION FROM MARKET GROWTH TO MATURITY

    A. Characteristics of the transition period

        1. Excess capacity

        2. More intense competition

        3. Difficulty of maintaining differentiation

        4. Distribution problems

        5. Pressures on costs and profits

    B. Strategic traps during the transition period

IV. BUSINESS STRATEGIES FOR MATURE MARKETS

    A. Strategies for maintaining competitive advantage

    B. Methods of differentiation

        1. Dimensions of product quality

        2. Dimensions of service quality

        3. Improving customer perceptions of service quality

    C. Methods for maintaining a low-cost position

        1. A no-frills product

        2. Innovative product design

        3. Cheaper raw materials

C. Marketing strategies for remaining competitors
    1. Harvesting strategy
    2. Maintenance strategy
    3. Profitable survivor strategy
    4. Niche strategy

VII. SUMMARY

ANSWERS TO DISCUSSION QUESTIONS

1. **Throughout the 1980s and into the 1990s, Delta was perceived to be a leader within the U. S. commercial airline industry in terms of service quality and customer satisfaction. What dimensions of service quality could Delta have emphasized to differentiate itself from competing airlines? What marketing actions would the firm have to take to reinforce and promote a high service quality image?**

Dimensions	*Marketing Actions*
• Tangibles	—Design and maintain attractive, clean airplane interiors, airport lounge areas, etc.
	—Design and maintain attractive, professional-looking uniforms for all personnel
	—Strive to serve high quality meals, movies, etc., relative to competitors
• Reliability	—Develop procedures to achieve high percentage of on-time departures and arrivals
	—Maintain highest possible service standards and safety record
	—Develop baggage-handling systems and procedures to speed deliver and minimize lost luggage
• Responsiveness	—Work to continually improve customer service standards and procedures
	—Train flight attendants/agents to provide good service
	—Evaluate and reward flight attendants/agents on basis of customer service performance
• Assurance	—Train pilots/flight attendants/agents/mechanics to improve and maintain high knowledge & skill levels
	—Utilize available technology (e.g., computers, etc.) to help improve employee performance
	—Train flight attendants/agents in customer contact protocols
• Empathy	—Train, evaluate, and reward customer-contact employees to encourage attention to individual customer needs
	—Advertise and promote employee friendliness and service (e.g., "We love to fly and it shows")

2. **Savin is one of the lowest cost producers in the office copier industry, even though its market share and production volume is smaller than the industry leader Xerox. How is it possible for a relatively small volume producer to achieve a low delivered cost position?**

Savin achieved its lower cost position by: (1) designing a simpler, "no-frills" line of copiers with fewer moving parts, (2) relying on standardized, off-the-shelf components; many of which are interchangeable across multiple models in the product line, (3) developing more efficient production processes (including, but not limited to, lower Japanese labor costs), (4) utilizing lower cost distribution channels (i.e., relying on independent office equipment dealers rather than developing vertically integrated channels like Xerox), and (5) holding down overhead costs, including sales and marketing expenses.

3. **Suppose you were the marketing manager for General Foods' Cool Whip frozen dessert topping during the late 1970s. Marketing research indicates that nearly three quarters of all households use your product, but the average user only buys it four times a year and Cool Whip is used on only seven percent of all toppable desserts. What marketing strategy (or strategies) would you recommend and why? What specific marketing actions would you propose to implement that strategy?**

Because of the high level of penetration of the target market, an *extended use* strategy should be the primary strategy pursued.

- Increase frequency of use among current users by:
  — Offering larger package sizes (but not *too* large because product is perishable)
  — Promotions to encourage larger/more frequent purchases (e.g., multi-pack deals, in-pack coupons good for next purchase)
  — Reminder advertising

- Encourage wider variety of uses among current users by:
  — Develop and promote new recipes and application (e.g., Cool Whip as an ingredient in pies, salads, etc.)
  — Tie-in promotions with complementary products (e.g., Jello, etc.)

There may also be opportunities for a *market expansion* strategy focused on untapped or under-developed segments.

- Expansion into global markets
- Lower-priced flanker brand to appeal to price-sensitive consumers
- Lower-calorie product for the weight-conscious segment
- Cool Whip with real cream

67

4. **During the 1980s and into the 1990s, McDonalds—who had attained several decades of outstanding growth by selling burgers and fries to American families with young children—aggressively sought franchises in foreign countries, including Russia and China. The firm also introduced a wide variety of new product lines and line extensions (e.g., breakfast items like Egg McMuffin and hash brown potatoes, salads, Chicken McNuggets, McChicken sandwiches, etc.). What was the strategic rationale for these moves?**

Growth was slowing in McDonalds traditional market segment due to (1) aging of the population, (2) extensive coverage of available geographic territories in the domestic market, (3) health concerns about consumption of fats, red meats, etc., and (4) increased competition. Thus, many of McDonalds' actions were aimed at extending volume growth in its maturing industry by:

- Extended use among current customers

    —Increasing traffic in off-peak periods (e.g., addition of new breakfast and lunch items)
    —New products & line extensions to increase use as customers' tastes change

- Market expansion by appealing to untapped or underdeveloped segments

    —Salads and chicken items for health and calorie-conscious adults

5. **The J.B. Kunz Corporation, the leading manufacturer of passbooks for financial institutions, saw its market gradually decline during the 1970s and 1980s because the switch to electronic banking was making its product superfluous. Nevertheless, the firm bought up the assets of a number of smaller competitors, greatly increased its market share within its industry, and managed to earn a very high return on investment. What kind of strategy was the company pursuing? Why do you think the firm was able to achieve a high ROI in the face of industry decline?**

The firm pursued a *profitable survivor* strategy. While market decline was certain, it happened at a slow and steady pace. Because Kunz had few strong competitors, and those competitors were also able to forecast a declining market, the firm was able to acquire their assets at favorable prices. By reducing the number of competitors in the industry and consolidating their assets, product lines, and marketing activities, Kunz was able to reduce price competition as well as operating and marketing costs. Thus, it could sustain—or even increase—its margins in the face of falling demand.

SUPPLEMENTARY REFERENCES:

See Footnotes 4, 6, 7, 9, 10, 12, 13, 14, 15, 21 29, 31

TRANSPARENCIES:

Chapter exhibits for which transparency masters prepared: 1, 3, 4, 5, 6, 7, 9, 14

CHAPTER 12
IMPLEMENTING BUSINESS AND MARKETING STRATEGIES

I.   HEWLETT-PACKARD: A MUCH ADMIRED COMPANY

II. ISSUES IN THE IMPLEMENTATION OF BUSINESS AND MARKETING STRATEGIES

    A. Relationships between business and marketing strategies

    B. Administrative relationships and strategy implementation

        1. Business unit autonomy

        2. Shared programs and facilities

        3. Evaluation and reward systems

III. ORGANIZATIONAL STRUCTURE, PROCESSES, AND STRATEGY IMPLEMENTATION

    A. Functional competencies and resource allocation

    B. Additional considerations for service organizations

IV. ORGANIZATIONAL STRUCTURES

    A. Functional organizations

    B. Product management organizations

    C. Process improvement

    D. Self-management teams

    E. Organizational design and the international company

        1. Little or no organization

        2. An international division

        3. Global structures

        4. Decision making and organizational structure

V. MARKETING ACTION PLANS

    A. Preparing the action plan

    B. Sections of a typical marketing plan

        1. Analysis of the current situation

        2. Market situation

        3. Competitive situation

        4. Macroenvironmental situation

        5. Past product performance

        6. Key issues

        7. Objectives

        8. Marketing strategy

        9. Action plans

        10. Projected profit-and-loss statement

VI. SUMMARY

ANSWERS TO DISCUSSION QUESTIONS

1. **What kinds of marketing strategies are most likely to be pursued by individual product-market entries within a low-cost defender SBU operating in a mature industry? Explain why you would expect to find this kind of consistent relationship between business and marketing strategies within most successful business units.**

   Common marketing strategies—fortress defense; confrontation, profitable survivor, maintenance strategy; niche strategy, harvesting strategy.

   Because specific product-market strategies most relevant for specific sets of market and competitive conditions are also likely to be more appropriate within a limited range of business-level competitive strategies as well.

2. **If you were the marketing director of the SBU described in question 1, what marketing policies would you establish to guide decisions concerning the business' products, prices, distribution channels and promotional programs? Explain the rationale for those policies.**

   Product and service policies—narrow, less technically sophisticated product lines; relatively low level and quality of service; maintain cost advantage.

   Price policy—relatively low to competitive prices; maintain price advantage.

   Distribution policy—degree of forward vertical integration indeterminant; low trade promotion expenses as a percent of sales; maintain cost advantage.

   Promotion policy—low advertising/sales promotion; and salesforce expenditure as a percent of sales; maintain cost advantage.

3. **How should the marketing policies for a differentiated defender SBU differ from those described in answering question 2? What is the rationale for those differences?**

   Product and service policies—high quality and technically sophisticated product lines; high quality and levels of service; maintain competitive advantage.

   Price policy—relatively high price; maintain perceived quality advantage.

   Distribution policy—relatively high degree of forward vertical integration; low trade promotion as a percent of sales; maintain control of distribution.

   Promotion policy—relatively low advertising and sales promotion as a percent of sales; high salesforce expenditure as a percent of sales; products require one-on-one promotional activity.

4. Suppose you have been offered the job of developing and managing a new medical products unit for a major electronics manufacturer. The purpose of the new SBU will be to adapt technology from other parts of the company for medical applications (e.g., diagnostic equipment such as CAT scanners, surgical lasers, etc.) and to identify and build markets for the new products the unit develops. The new unit's performance over the next several years will be judged primarily on its success of developing a variety of new products and its rate of growth in sales volume and market share. Before accepting the job, what assurances would you seek from the company's CEO concerning the administrative relationships to be established between the new SBU and corporate headquarters? Why?

Two key issues would need to be addressed, given the delineation of evaluation already identified. One involves the autonomy which the new unit will have relative to other units in the organization. The manager should be promised a relatively high level of autonomy in order to make the decisions necessary to develop new products. The second issue is the amount of shared programs and synergy which will exist between the new unit and other SBUs in the company. The manager should insist on relatively little required synergy between units in order to have the ability to develop its own marketing and R&D programs.

5. Now that you have accepted the job described in question 4, you have been given a $50 million operating budget for the first year. Your first task is to staff the new unit and to allocate your budget across its various functional departments. While you obviously want to hire good people for every position, which departments require the most competent and experienced personnel, and which departments should receive relatively large shares of the available budget? Why?

The first place to start would be with a good R&D department which would be able to generate product ideas using the technology within the other organizational SBUs. This would require hiring good medical technicians and perhaps a few doctors to help in the R&D process. In addition, the manager should hire some experienced salespeople to test the market for ideas.

6. As general manger, what type of organizational design would you select for the new SBU described in question 4? Justify your choice in terms of its ability to help the SBU implement its strategy and accomplish its primary objectives. What potential advantages—if any—might be associated with your chosen organization structure?

Given the complexity of the products and the apparent scope of the new SBU's product offerings, a product management structure would probably be most appropriate. The reason for this is that it would allow managers to concentrate their efforts on developing a broad range of products at the same time as each manager is responsible for his/her own product development and marketing approaches. A possible alternative would be a matrix or team structure for product development, switching to product managers as those products become established.

SUPPLEMENTARY REFERENCES:

See Footnotes 5, 6, 15, 21,25, 34

TRANSPARENCIES:

Chapter exhibits for which transparency masters prepared: 2, 3, 4, 8

CHAPTER 13
CONTROLLING MARKETING STRATEGIES AND PROGRAMS

VII. CONTINGENCY PLANNING

      A. Identifying critical assumptions

      B. Assigning probabilities

      C. Rank ordering the critical assumptions

      D. Tracking and monitoring

      E. Activating contingency plan

      F. Specifying response options

VIII. SUMMARY

ANSWERS TO DISCUSSIN QUESTIONS

1. **The control system at Wal-Mart is an important reason for their success. Specifically, how has this system helped them become the largest retailer in the world?**

   Wal-Mart's control system has been a major reason why the company is the low-cost leader in its industry. By being able to convert information into action almost immediately, it can control and automatically replenish its inventories; track sales by stockkeeping unit, product groupings, departments, stores, district, and regions; determine whether the seven-second credit card approval system is working properly, distribute messages to the entire system with but a few minutes notice, determine whether Wal-Mart continues to be the low-priced discounter and take advantage of new merchandise opportunities. By merging state-of-the-art computer communications technology with hands-on management, Wal-Mart has developed a distribution system which is the envy of the industry.

2. **MTS Systems, Inc., is a relatively small manufacturer of measurement instruments used to monitor and control automated production processes in a number of different industries, such as the automotive and aerospace industries. The firm has a company salesforce of 12 people, each of whom calls on companies in a particular industry. While the firm's sales have increased steadily in recent years, its profits have been relatively stagnant. One problem is that the firm has no information concerning the relative profitability of the various products it makes or the different customers it sells to. MTS Systems has hired you as a marketing consultant to design a *control system* that will enable the firm to evaluate its performance across the various items in its product line and the various segments of its market. Outline the major steps of activities you would recommend including in such a control system.**

   1. set performance standards based on corporate objectives

   2. specify and obtain feedback data

   3. evaluate the data

   4. take corrective action (if necessary)

3. **What specific types of *information* would have to be collected and evaluated in order to implement the control system you outlined in your answer to question 2? What sources could be used to obtain each necessary type of information?**

Types of information—(1) sales analysis for each salesperson, which could be drawn from invoices and other internally generated information; (2) profitability per order, again taken from invoices and internal cost information; (3) customer information about size of customer base and which customers generate the most business, drawn from customer records; (4) product information about which products are most profitable and which are the biggest sellers, drawn from invoice information.

4. **Discuss the relative advantages and limitation of the *full costing versus the contribution margin* approaches for determining the profitability of a specific item within a firm's product line. Which approach do you think is most commonly used by large, multi-SBU corporations? Why?**

Full costing—analysts assign both direct or variable and indirect costs to the unit of analysis. Direct costs are directly associated with the unit of analysis (production costs, direct marketing costs). Indirect costs involve certain fixed joint costs that cannot be linked directly to a single unit of analysis (general management, costs of occupying a facility).

Contribution margin—this approach argues that there is really no accurate way to assign indirect costs. In addition, because indirect costs are mostly fixed costs, a product or market may make a contribution to profits even if it shows a loss. Thus, even though overhead must eventually be absorbed, the contribution method clearly indicates what is gained by adding or dropping a product or customer.

Large, multi-SBU corporations would most probably use a contribution margin approach, since it enables the firm to better assess the way a product adds or subtracts from overall profitability.

5. **You are a marketing manager in an SBU of a large consumer food manufacturer. The SBU's general manager has asked you to conduct a *marketing audit* of the SBU as a basis for evaluating its strategic and operational strengths and weaknesses. What issues or areas of concern should be covered by your audit?**

    1. the marketing environment

    2. objectives and strategy

    3. planning and control system

    4. organization

    5. marketing productivity

    6. marketing functions

6. **For each set of issues to be included in the audit you designed in your answer to question 5, specify the kinds of information you would need to collect and the major sources you might use to obtain that information.**

    1. *Marketing environment*—what opportunities and/or threats derive from the firm's present and future environment: that is, what technological, political, and social trends are significant? Sources—news magazines, government publications.

    2. *Objectives and strategy*—how logical are the company's objectives, given the more significant opportunities/threats and its relative resources? How valid is the firm's strategy, given the anticipated environment? Sources—internal company strategic documents.

    3. *Planning and control system*—does the firm have adequate and timely information about consumers' satisfaction with the products? With the actions of competitors? Sources—internal marketing information system.

    4. *Organization*—does the organization structure fit the evolving needs of the marketplace?

    5. *Marketing productivity*—how profitable are each of the firm's products/brands? How effective are each of the firm's marketing activities? Sources—internal company cost and marketing documents (invoices).

    6. *Marketing functions*—how well does the product line meet the unit's objectives? How well do the other marketing mix elements fit corporate objectives? Sources—internal company documents.

7. When they say the result of the *sales territory analysis* presented in Exhibit 13-4, the firm's top managers concluded that Barlow in territory 1 was not devoting sufficient effort to her job, since her performance was more than $32,000 below quota. They have asked you—the firm's sales manager—to have a talk with Barlow and suggest ways to improve her performance. Do you agree that Barlow's performance is probably the result of too little effort on her part? Why or why not?

It is difficult without further information to say for certain what is the cause of Barlow not reaching her quota. On her behalf, she is fairly close to reaching her quota (94%). This might suggest that perhaps a little more effort would put her over the top. However, there might be other reasons (more training, personal reasons, etc.). It is also possible that her quota was set too high in view of competitive conditions or other uncontrollable factors.

8. What other causes might be responsible for Barlow's failure to make her quota? What additional information or analyses would you seek in order to determine what should be done to improve Barlow's future performance?

1. customer analysis—an analysis of Barlow's customers to determine if she is doing a good job of qualifying her customers.

2. product analysis—what is the mix of products she is selling? Perhaps she needs to sell a different mix of product combinations.

3. order size—how big is an average order? Perhaps she needs to work on putting together larger orders.

4. analysis of competitive actions in Barlow's territories.

SUPPLEMENTARY REFERENCES:

See Footnotes 5, 6, 11, 14

TRANSPARENCIES:

Chapter exhibits for which transparency masters prepared: 1, 4, 5, 7, 8, 9, 11A, 11B, 12, 14

TRANSPARENCY MASTERS FOR THE INTRODUCTORY SESSION

1. CALGOLIA, INC., LISTING OF TRANSPARENCIES

2. SITUATION

3. SELECTED INTERNATIONAL MARKETING STRATEGY ISSUES

4. LEVELS OF MARKETING STRATEGY

5. MARKETING ANALYSIS AND STRATEGY

6. MARKET ANALYSIS BY PRODUCT CATEGORIES

7. MARKET ANALYSIS BY COUNTRIES

8. COMPANY ANALYSIS BY PRODUCT CATEGORIES

9. COMPANY ANALYSIS BY COUNTRIES

10. COMPANY ANALYSIS — PROFIT STRUCTURE BY PRODUCT CATEGORIES

11. COMPANY ANALYSIS — PROFIT STRUCTURE BY COUNTRIES

12. SUMMARY OF ANALYSIS

13. A FEW OPERATIONAL NUMBERS

14. YOUR CHALLENGE

SITUATION

- **Ms. Sylvia Retchi, European Marketing Manager**

- **3 Product Categories: Ovadols, Squazols, Trigols**

- **5 Countries: United Kingdom, Poland, France, Germany, Italy**

- **Greater International Coordination Wanted**

- **Broad 10-Year Projection**

- **Maximize Shareholder Value**

CALGOLIA Inc.

SELECTED INTERNATIONAL MARKETING STRATEGY ISSUES

•**Global Allocation of Marketing Resources**

Management Time Consumer Marketing Trade Marketing	→	3 Product Categories 5 Countries

•**Global Standardization vs. Local Adaptation of:**

- •Pricing
- •Product Specifications
- •Consumer Marketing
- •Trade Marketing

•**Organization & People**

Management Team

LEVELS OF MARKETING STRATEGY

OBJECTIVE

- Maximization of Shareholder Value/Share Price

PORTFOLIO STRATEGY

- Allocation of Resources Between
  - Products
  - Markets

PRODUCT MARKET STRATEGY

- Market Segmentation

- Product Positioning

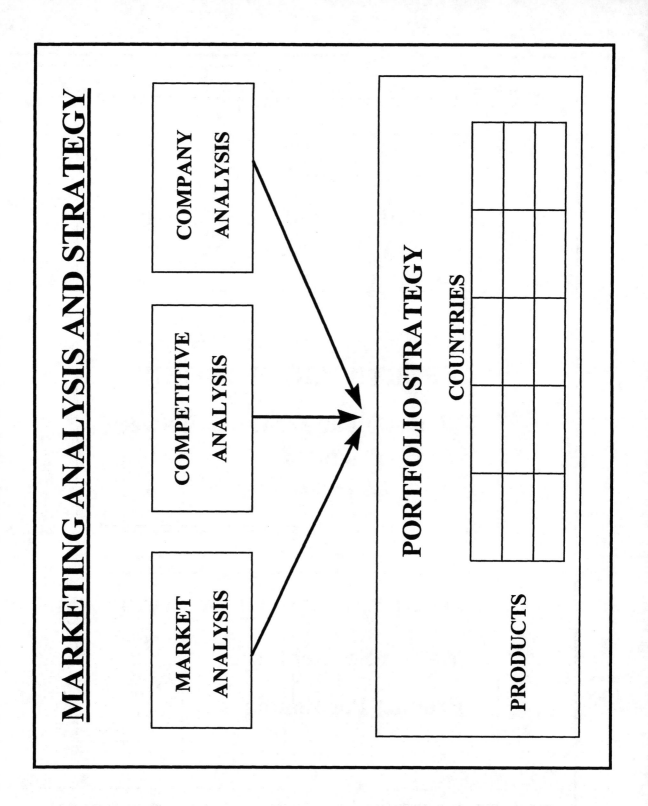

MARKET ANALYSIS

	PRODUCT CATEGORIES			
	OVADOLS	SQUAZOLS	TRIGOLS	
Category Situation				
• Current Size (MS)	409	233	291	
• Stage in life cycle	Maturing	High Growth	Growth/Maturing	
• Long term growth	6%	14%	10%	
Difference between countries				
• In product purpose	Moderate	Low	Moderate	
• In consumer profiles	Moderate	High	Moderate	
• In price levels	Low	High	Moderate	
• In trade demand	Moderate	High	Low	
Competition				
• Number of international firms	5	3	4	
• Evolution	Stable	Unstable	Consolidating	
• MS of largest competitor	17%	15%	13%	
CALGOLIA Situation				
• Reputation	Strong	Strong	Weak	
• MS (based on $)	13.9%	18.9%	7.5%	
• Worldwide position	No. 2	No. 1	No. 4	

MARKET ANALYSIS

COUNTRIES

	UNITED KINGDOM	POLAND	FRANCE	GERMANY	ITALY
ECONOMIC SITUATION					
• Population	57M	38M	57M	81M	58M
• Income level	Medium	Low	Medium	High	Medium
• Trade Concentration	High	Low	Medium	Medium	Low
RELEVANT CATEGORIES					
• Current size (M$)	265	115	152	214	187
• Long term growth	6%	15%	10%	13%	11%
• Price Sensitivity	Low	Moderate	Low	Moderate	Moderate
• Sophistication	High	Low	High	Medium	Low
COMPETITION					
• Number of local firms	3	12	7	6	9
• Number of international firms (incl. CALGOLIA)	6	2	4	3	2
• MS of largest competitor	15%	10%	15%	17%	16%
• Evolution	Stable	Dormant	Unstable	Consolidating	Dormant
• Price Pressures	High	Low	High	Medium	Low
CALGOLIA SITUATION					
• History	Longer established	Early entry	Long established	Long established	Recent entry
• MS (based on $)	12.3%	15.6%	10.4%	14.6%	13.5%
• Overall strength	No. 2	No. 1	No. 4	No. 2	No. 3

COMPANY ANALYSIS - MARKETING

PRODUCT CATEGORIES

	OVADOLS	SQUAZOLS	TRIGOLS
MS (%$)	13.9%	18.9%	7.5%
Revenue (%)	46%	36%	18%
CAM (%)	46%	41%	13%
Marketing Resources (%)	40%	35%	26%
CM/Total Marketing (%)	64%	62%	67%
Management Priority (%)	33%	33%	33%
Local Adaptation			
• Product	90	15	40
• Consumer Marketing	60	40	20
• Trade Marketing	90	30	30
• Price Variation (%)	12	23	19

COMPANY ANALYSIS - MARKETING

COUNTRIES

	UNITED KINGDOM	POLAND	FRANCE	GERMANY	ITALY
MS (%$) Revenues (%) CAM (%)	12.3% 27% 23%	15.6% 15% 14%	10.4% 13% 11%	14.6% 25% 29%	13.5% 21% 23%
Marketing Resources (%) CM/Total Marketing (%)	30% 65%	14% 64%	16% 65%	22% 64%	19% 65%

COMPANY ANALYSIS–PROFIT STRUCTURE

(% Revenues)

	PRODUCT CATEGORIES		
	OVADOLS	SQUAZOLS	TRIGOLS
Revenues	100.0	100.0	100.0
CBM	60.4	68.0	66.6
Consumer Marketing	14.6	15.9	25.6
Trade Marketing	8.1	9.5	12.4
CAM	37.7	42.6	28.6

COMPANY ANALYSIS - PROFIT STRUCTURE
(% Revenues)

COUNTRIES

	UNITED KINGDOM	POLAND	FRANCE	GERMANY	ITALY
Revenues	100.0	100.0	100.00	100.0	100.0
CBM	62.6	60.9	64.7	65.6	66.8
Consumer Marketing	19.1	15.6	21.7	14.7	15.4
Trade Marketing	10.4	8.9	11.5	8.3	8.3
CAM	33.1	36.4	31.6	42.6	43.1

SUMMARY OF ANALYSIS

- **OVADOLS:**
  - Nearly Half of Revenues and CAM
  - Lowest Growth Opportunity
  - Highest Level of Local Adaptation, except for Price
  - Highest Consumer Product Satisfaction, Consumer Marketing and Trade Marketing Effectiveness
  - Lowest Marketing Intensity as % of Revenue

-

- **SQUAZOLS:**
  - Highest Growth Opportunity
  - Strongest Market Share Position
  - Highest Product Standardization
  - Highest Consumer Price Satisfaction

-

- **TRIGOLS:**
  - Middle Size and Growth
  - Weakest Market Share Position
  - Highest Marketing Intensity as % of Revenue

-

- **COUNTRIES:**
  - United Kingdom and Germany: Largest Size
  - Poland and Germany: Largest Growth Opportunities

- **PRICE PRESSURES**

THE GAMAR3 SIMULATION
A FEW OPERATIONAL NUMBERS

- Budget: Between 45m$ and 150m$
  Consumer and Trade Marketing

- Management Time: 360 man-months
  fixed cost, not out of CAM

- UVC = 100$ for Ovadols, 40$ for Squazols, 60$ for Trigols

- UVC Increase for Maximum Local Product Adaptation: 30%

- Maximum Price Differential = 30% between lowest and
  highest prices of same product
  in different countries

- Maximum Consumer or Trade Marketing Budget =
  15m$ for a given product in a given country

YOUR CHALLENGE

- •69 Decisions/Period for 10 Periods

- •10 Possible Tests per Period

STRATEGY

vs.

BUNCH OF DECISIONS

vs.

EXPERIMENTATION

vs.

RANDOM WALK

?

CALGOLIA INC.

Towards a strategic approach to international marketing

Instructor's Notes

OVERVIEW

TEACHING WITH THE CALGOLIA CASE

TEACHING THE INTRODUCTORY SESSION

THE CALGOLIA ASSIGNMENT

TEACHING THE CONCLUDING SESSION

EXHIBITS

    A: The GAMAR3 simulation
    B: CALGOLIA in undergraduate or graduate courses
    C: CALGOLIA in executive seminars
    D: Example of an "Excellent" GAMAR3 plan
    E: Transparency masters for the introductory session

CALGOLIA INC.

Towards a strategic approach to international marketing

INSTRUCTOR'S NOTES

OVERVIEW

The **CALGOLIA** package deals with selected marketing issues at three levels: international marketing, strategic marketing, and the marketing mix. Thus, the instructor can use it as an integrative teaching tool, or concentrate on those aspects which are most appropriate for a part of his or her course.

The package is composed of the CALGOLIA case and the GAMAR3 simulation. The case can be used without the simulation, which allows students to manage an international firm on the computer and to test many of the concepts learned during a marketing course. The whole simulation can be run effectively in less than a few hours. Instructors who have previously been discouraged from using other simulations because of the time involved, the high set-up costs, or the computer sophistication will find the CALGOLIA package very easy to use.

This learning tool is a major revision of the GAMAR case and has benefited from the comments of many past users. Some of its main features are:

1. A clear separation of the case and the simulation. Part I of the case can be used independently before or without the use of the simulation. The separation is reinforced by the use of different names for the company described in the case and for the simulation.

2. The consideration of five real countries—United Kingdom, Germany, France, Italy, and Poland—as the relevant international market. These countries offer different marketing situations while still representing potential opportunities.

3. Four levels of difficulties in the simulation—Basic, Intermediate, Advanced, and Expert— allow the instructor to adapt the tool to the level and the objectives of the class. The Basic level with only one product category in two countries provides a good challenge for students in an undergraduate marketing management class!

4. An Analysis module in the simulation which integrates selected information and helps students to concentrate on Key Performance Indicators.

5. A graphical representation of the Growth–Share matrix shows the relative position of each product category in each country. In testing the simulation, it proved to be helpful to students in addressing the issue of allocating scarce marketing resources.

6. A Resources Allocation Strategy module helps students set strategic guidelines for allocating resources as opposed to having to make each individual decision. This has been found to improve the motivation of students, their concentration on strategic issues, and the quality of their results.

7. A Global Price Change module helps students set guidelines for pricing decisions as opposed to making individual decisions. This should improve the students' decision-making process.

TEACHING WITH THE CALGOLIA PACKAGE

The **CALGOLIA** package includes both the case and the GAMAR3 simulation. The case describes the situation faced by the European Marketing Manager of a North American multinational firm. It offers students a unique opportunity to debate a number of general marketing concepts in a global context. More specifically, three main issues are raised in the case:

1. **The Marketing Mix. CALGOLIA** includes several marketing mix elements: product, price, consumer marketing, and trade marketing. It helps students to improve their understanding of the different role of various marketing tools, of how the effectiveness of each tool varies over the product life cycle, and of the interaction between these tools.

2. **Strategic Marketing.** Beyond the specification of the mix for a given product, and the allocation of funds between alternate instruments such as consumer and trade marketing, the existence of a product portfolio offers a higher level of strategic consideration. In **CALGOLIA**, students must determine guidelines for the short and long term allocation of marketing resources between three product categories, Trigols, Ovadols, and Squazols, which are in different markets and competitive situations.

3. **International Marketing.** The two issues described above concern any marketing situation, and especially domestic marketing, traditionally the implicit reference. The **CALGOLIA** package broadens students' perspective beyond this traditional "mono-territory" approach which is even less representative of modern management challenges. **CALGOLIA** concentrates on the two main strategic issues of international marketing: the allocation of resources among countries, and the extent to which marketing elements should be standardized globally, or on the contrary adapted to local conditions. More specialized and tactical issues such as exchange rates, exports, regulations, or local partnering are not addressed in order to concentrate on strategic issues.

These issues are difficult to teach effectively in the static environment of a traditional case. A computerized simulation is the most appropriate way to illustrate both the effects of the marketing mix and the dynamics of marketing resource allocation. In a simulation, students manage a firm over a period of time and, in an iterative process, they analyze, make decisions, receive rapid feedback, and adjust their strategies over time. The teaching effectiveness of strategic marketing simulations such as MARKSTRAT[1] is now widely documented. They have become an important component of Marketing Management and Marketing Strategy courses.

The **CALGOLIA** package combines the limited time demands of a case study with the learning dynamics of a simulation. It gives the instructor the opportunity to expose students to an integrative simulation without allocating a significant portion of the course to the exercise since it can be used outside the class as a team project or as part of the course over one to three sessions.

The **CALGOLIA** package is designed to offer a great deal of flexibility to the instructor. By changing the emphasis on its three main learning dimensions (marketing mix, product portfolio strategies, international issues), it can be included in courses on Marketing Principles, Marketing Management, Marketing Strategy, or International Marketing. Similarly, it is attractive to a broad audience, whether inexperienced undergraduates, MBA students, managers from local to medium-sized firms, or executives from large multinational corporations. Extensive use of the learning package in executive seminars shows that it generates as much enthusiasm from young product managers as from experienced vice presidents and CEOs.

Teaching **CALGOLIA** usually involves three basic steps:

Step 1.   **Introductory session.** This is a class session in which the case is discussed before the simulation is used. The session's main purpose is to make sure that all students are aware of the various issues involved and of related marketing concepts. This session also gives the instructor the opportunity to be in full control of the exercise. Depending on the teaching environment, he or she may decide to present the role of the exercise in the overall course, to set up teams, to offer hints about learning processes or effective strategies, to review schedules and logistics, or to give a demo of the software.

Step 2.   **Student Assignment.** Individually, or in teams, students develop a marketing plan for CALGOLIA. This involves formulating strategies which are then tested, modified, and refined with the help of the GAMAR3 simulation. The assignment can be carried out in a minimum of two hours in a time-constrained executive seminar. As a home assignment, an average student can formulate and finalize an excellent marketing plan in less than five hours.

---

[1]See Jean-Claude Larréché and Hubert Gatignon, MARKSTRAT3: The **Strategic Marketing Simulation,** Cincinnati, Ohio, South-Western College Publishing, 1997. The CALGOLIA case has also been used as a complement to MARKSTRAT3 to emphasize the issues related to international marketing.

Step 3.   **Concluding Session.** Depending on time constraints, this can involve a whole session or only part of one. It typically includes a comparison of the results achieved by different members of the class, student presentations and discussions, as well as guidelines for good strategies.

These three steps constitute an adequate teaching plan for most courses. Many other approaches are possible, however, to fit a variety of teaching situations. At one extreme, an instructor may decide not to allocate CALGOLIA any class time and to give it strictly as a home assignment. At the other extreme, another may give CALGOLIA much more importance and reiterate the above steps several times during a course.

The following pages describe the three components of the CALGOLIA learning process: the introductory session, the assignment, and the concluding session. The exhibits include additional hints on the GAMAR3 simulation software; suggestions for organizing the learning experience in three situations—using CALGOLIA strictly as a project or home assignment, as an integral part of a regular course, or in an executive seminar; an example of a good strategy; and teaching aids with transparency masters for classroom use.

TEACHING THE INTRODUCTORY SESSION

While brief, the CALGOLIA case contains a wealth of information and data concentrated in just four exhibits. One purpose of the case is to illustrate the importance of a systematic process in extracting important information from a mass of available data, in organizing it, and in identifying clear strategic options. Discussion of the CALGOLIA case will usually involve several steps:

1. Sylvia Retchi's Challenge

2. Market Analysis

3. Company Analysis

4. Summary of Analysis

5. Conclusions

Transparencies can be used in this session either to drive the discussion or simply to sum it up. Masters for the transparencies used by the author in this session are referred to in the discussion below. They are included in Exhibit 10 (which can be found at the end of this Instructor's Manual) and refer to the highest level of difficulty in the simulation. This level, named "Expert," includes all three product categories and all five countries. It will be the level considered throughout these notes. All observations are equally valid for lower levels of difficulty which, while less complex, have access to smaller resources and face similar issues of allocation standardization and adaptation.

1. What is the challenge for Sylvia Retchi?

The first three transparencies address three different ways of approaching this question:

The situation

As European Marketing Manager, Sylvia has to develop a 10-year projection for CALGOLIA's three top product categories in five major countries. The objective is clearly to maximize shareholder value by the end of the year 2007, as measured by the Share Price Index estimated by the simulation.

International marketing issues

Key international issues facing Sylvia are the global allocation of marketing resources, global standardization versus local adaptation of the marketing mix, and organization of people (this refers to possible conflicts between headquarters and subsidiaries as well as to competition between subsidiaries for resources, influence, and power). Students may wonder whether these issues are relevant since the case gives no information on these aspects. They are first implicit in Period 0 decisions and the instructor may want to generate a discussion on how organizational or people issues can lead to suboptimal marketing strategies. The other way in which this dimension dramatically comes to life is within the teams involved in the simulation themselves. It is amazing how problems experienced by large multinationals are already apparent in groups of a half-dozen students! This discussion can take place either in the introductory session or in the concluding one, after better decisions have been formulated.

Levels of marketing strategy

This transparency positions Sylvia's highest strategic concern in terms of maximizing shareholder value and strategy for a portfolio of products and countries. It also makes the point that the level of marketing strategy concerned with market segmentation and product positioning is not explicitly addressed in the CALGOLIA case.

At this point, two approaches can be used to open the discussion further:

- A *result-oriented* approach: In which order of priority would you rank the three product categories for CALGOLIA? In which order of priority would you order the five countries? Or, more provocatively, If you had to get out of a product category, which one would you choose? If you had to get out of two countries, which ones would they be?

- A *process-oriented* approach: What process would you follow to decide how to allocate marketing resources between the three key product categories and the five major countries?

The results of these two approaches will be fairly similar and both will lead to a discussion of the issues presented below. The first approach tends to create a more lively discussion but makes it more difficult to keep an orderly board plan. In any case, at some point in the discussion, a process should emerge.

The next transparency, on Marketing Analysis and Strategy, emphasizes the three pillars of marketing analysis (market, competition, and the firm) which need to be reviewed before formulating a strategy. The point can be made at this time that, in the CALGOLIA exercise, competition is treated at the aggregate level for the sake of simplicity, and its impact is implicit in the market's response to the firm's actions. This sets the stage for the next phase of the discussion.

2. Market Analysis

The next two transparencies show selected aspects of the evolution of the three product categories and the five countries. They are based on Exhibits 1 to 4 of the case. Several key points emerge from this marketing analysis:

- Ovadols have the largest market, followed by Trigols and Squazols. The ranking in terms of growth opportunities is exactly the reverse, with the projected growth for Squazols double that for Ovadols;
- The United Kingdom and Germany are the largest countries followed by Italy, France, and Poland. Poland has the highest projected growth rate followed by Germany, Italy, and France. The United Kingdom has by far the lowest growth prospects;
- Downward pressures on price are anticipated in most countries, but especially in the United Kingdom and France.

The discussion may cover many other aspects and students will have a better feel for market dynamics when they use the simulation to test alternate decisions. It is, however, important that they have this broad market perspective clearly in mind before using the simulation. Finally, it should be emphasized that the projections should be used only for what they are. While these projections are the best current estimates, students should realize that their decisions will have an impact on the behavior of both the market and competitors. As a result, future market growth rates and prices will be influenced by the firm's decisions and the projections may not always materialize.

3. Company Analysis

The next four transparencies deal with an analysis of CALGOLIA's marketing position and profit structure. Nearly half its revenues and CAM (Contribution After Marketing) are generated by Ovadols, with Squazols also a strong contributor. Trigols' CAM is less than a third of Ovadols', but Trigols nonetheless play a significant role in CALGOLIA's portfolio.

103

CALGOLIA's market share varies widely across the three product categories. Its strongest position, with 18.9%, is for Squazols which also enjoy the highest growth rate. The weakest position is in Trigols with 7.5%.

Trigols receive a higher proportion of marketing resources than its current revenues or CAM would justify. This would indicate that CALGOLIA is trying to catch up in this category by investing heavily. Ovadols on the contrary command a proportionally lower level of the amount spent on marketing. The split of marketing expenditures between Consumer Marketing (CM) and Trade Marketing (TM) appears to be approximately the same in all categories. Management Time is equally allocated between the three products.

Ovadols enjoy the highest level of local adaptation, probably reflecting the fact that they were developed in an era of international decentralization, but have the lowest level of price variation between countries. Squazols, the most recent category, has the highest level of global product standardization. Trigols overall are in an intermediate situation of local adaptation, except for consumer marketing where they present the highest degree of standardization.

CALGOLIA's total market share across the five countries varies from 10.4% to 15.6%. One has to be careful in this type of aggregation, but these numbers reflect the power of CALGOLIA in each country relative to its competitors and to the trade. CALGOLIA's position is strongest in Poland and France, the countries with the highest growth projections, reflecting wise choices made by the firm in the past. There is definitely a hierarchy in the countries' relative importance to CALGOLIA. This hierarchy is not exactly the same in terms of revenues or CAM, but the United Kingdom, Germany, and Italy have much more weight than the other two countries. However, even the smallest country requires some serious consideration as it represents a non-negligible proportion of CALGOLIA's revenues or CAM.

The global profit structure for each product category is quite different. Contribution Before Marketing (CBM) ranges from 60.4% of revenues for Ovadols to 68.0% for Squazols. This difference, stemming directly from the price level relative to unit variable costs, means that an extra 7.6% of revenues could be spent on marketing Squazols compared to Ovadols, for the same CAM objective. The actual amount spent on marketing Squazols is indeed higher than for Ovadols, but only by 2.7%, resulting in a higher CAM level. Marketing expenditures as a percentage of sales is much higher for Trigols than for the other two products, reflecting an important effort made by CALGOLIA in this category. As a result, Trigols' CAM is substantially lower than that for Squazols or Ovadols.

Significant differences in profit structure also exist among countries. Italy has the highest CAM, mainly driven by a high CBM. France has the lowest CAM due to very high proportional investments in both Consumer and Trade Marketing. Two countries (Germany and

Italy) have much higher CAM than the others. It appears that the countries with the highest revenues also have the highest CAM, with the exception of the United Kingdom which has both a low CBM and high amounts spent on marketing. Does it make sense? This question can be answered by testing alternate approaches with the simulation.

4. Summary of Analysis

The next transparency summarizes the key points from the previous discussion. The objective is to present the main Opportunities, Threats, Strengths, and Weaknesses in order to facilitate the formulation of strategies by the students. Alternatively, this summary can be written on the board on the basis of students' comments. One will generally develop a feeling that:

- Trigols are the most difficult product category and probably require a "double or quit" approach;

- Ovadols should be made much more efficient and turned into a "cash cow" if their position is not too sensitive to a cut in the amount spent on marketing;

- Price pressures will require more efficient operations overall. The large level of local adaptation on the more mature categories may present some opportunities for rationalization through standardization, provided it does not prompt market reactions that are too negative;

- France appears the least attractive country when the dimensions of size, growth, market share and profitability are combined. It would be the prime candidate for "milking" or "divestment" should the need arise.

Many issues are still unresolved at this point, especially market sensitivity to various marketing instruments. This can only be hinted at based on initial market growth rates, market shares, and marketing investment levels. These issues can, however, be better understood by testing directly alternate approaches in the simulation. These broad observations should help students develop resource allocation strategies which can then be tested.

5. Final Recommendations

The last three transparencies of the introductory session include some final recommendations to students before they start the assignment. One concerns operational data scattered through the case which students risk overlooking. The second one recapitulates and refines the set objective of maximizing shareholder value. The example given is for a 4000 share price objective in 2007 which, as shown later in these notes, corresponds to the bottom of the "very good results" category. This corresponds to a compounded growth rate in value of 15% and, given a projected market growth rate of 11%, shows an annual growth gap of 4% which has to be bridged by improvements in marketing!

The final slide warns students against playing with the computer and trying to outsmart the model. There are 69 decisions per period, hence 690 decisions for the 10 periods, and the possible combinations go into trillions. This is a well-known situation to chess players and management scientists, but often overlooked by students and executives alike! Formulating guidelines and strategies dramatically reduces the number of actual decisions. The simplest strategy in this regard could be as follows:

- Standard cost-plus pricing for all products and markets: one decision;
- Constant rule for the allocation of management time and marketing budget between the 15 OMUs (Operating Market Units), proportional to market size: one decision;
- Constant and identical allocation between consumer and trade marketing for all OMUs: one decision;
- Constant and identical local adaptation for product, consumer marketing and trade marketing, for all OMUs: one decision.

In this case, 690 potential decisions have been reduced to 4! While this results in tremendous simplification, one should notice that the four remaining decisions are still quite difficult to make. In addition, the constraints set by these guidelines are probably too rigid to allow for an effective strategy. The point is, however, that students should not try to develop decisions randomly. The problem is too complex for them not to use their brains and knowledge. The 10 test runs allowed for each period, while taking up a considerable amount of time if they are all used, are only an infinitesimal fraction of all possible combinations. The challenge therefore is to formulate alternate strategies and to experiment in order to learn how successful they are and how they can be improved.

INSTRUCTIONS FOR THE CALGOLIA ASSIGNMENT

Students should put themselves in Sylvia Retchi's position. Their overall assignment, as stated in the case, is to formulate a long term international marketing strategy for CALGOLIA. The objective is clearly to maximize shareholder value as measured by the Share Price Index at the end of Period 10. Running "status quo projections" by replicating the same decisions for 10 periods would demonstrate a serious concern: while the share price index remains practically stable over the next 10 years, market share declines by about half. This is compensated for by a doubling of market size, resulting in flat total revenues. While these observations are based on an aggregation of all product categories and countries, and hence simplified, they put Sylvia's challenge into perspective. *One can estimate that just holding global market share would double the share price index over the next 10 years.*

Additional Directions

While the problem faced by Sylvia Retchi is well described in the case, the following additional directions and information should be given to students:

1. Which difficulty level has been selected for the assignment, between "Basic," "Intermediate," "Advanced," and "Expert." The choice should depend on the level of the class, the place in the course, and the time available. When a level has been selected, students may find it still useful to first try simpler levels first.

2. A total of two to five hours is adequate to complete the assignment (i.e., to formulate a complete international marketing plan, test it, and improve it with the GAMAR3 simulation). Two hours is tight and requires perfect logistics as well as available assistance, a situation often found in executive programs. In five hours, any student or group of students can, on average, develop a very good plan. This does not include any written report which the instructor may request. At the end of this time, students should have in hand a printout showing their results after Period 10.

3. Each student or group can make as many as 10 test runs of the simulation per period. After seeing the results for a given period, they can change the decisions and rerun it before moving forward to the next one. In addition, they may create a new firm and restart the simulation, a process which takes more time as decisions have to be re-entered for every period since Period 0. Given the combinatorial complexity of the simulation, one can always improve upon a given plan. Some students may be tempted to optimize the early periods and find themselves short of time to develop a proper plan for later periods. If given unlimited time, some students may put much more effort than they should into this assignment. A satisfactory guideline is that five test runs per period are sufficient to gain a good understanding of market behavior and to develop a good plan over the 10 periods. This obviously requires having first developed a basic plan and having a systematic approach to investigate specific issues. The upper limit of 10 test runs per period only provides more freedom.

4. Before starting working on the simulation, students should have developed clear guidelines for allocating resources among products and countries. A simple rank ordering of the relative importance of products and countries would be sufficient. Alternatively, students can be encouraged to classify products and countries into different strategic modes such as those found in the various portfolio tools (such as "invest," "double or quit," "sustain," "milk," or "divest"). The share–growth matrix in the Analysis module can be used for this purpose. Students can also be advised to think not only in terms of individual decisions but also in terms of guidelines (such as "x% of marketing on trade," "higher marketing investment in high growth situations," or "we will go for complete product standardization throughout and give consumers a lower price") in order to cope with the complexity of the decision set.

5. Students should not waste time printing out the results of each test run, as this could be a lengthy process. They are better off making a note of key figures and they always can display on the screen the detailed results of previous periods. They should, however, print their final report at the end of Period 10 and bring it to class for presentation and discussion.

6. While instructions to operate the GAMAR3 simulation are summarized in Appendix A of the case, it may be desirable for the instructor to demonstrate use of the software in class.

TEACHING THE CONCLUDING SESSION

This class discussion can take between half an hour (in which case it will be a simple debriefing of the simulation and conclusions with key messages) and one and a half hours (which allows for students' presentations and a full-fledged discussion). The following are guidelines for a full session. Each instructor can choose selected items for shorter sessions.

1. How well have you done?

First ask students for the Share Price Index they have achieved at the end of Period 10 and write it down on the board. If the assignment was given to teams, a typical class will include 5 to 12 teams, and full information can be gathered and displayed. If the number of teams is large, or if the exercise was assigned on an individual basis, it is preferable to obtain and display the lowest, highest, and median results. Obviously, if the assignment has been returned ahead of the class, a more complete analysis can be presented to the students. The distribution obtained for the class can be supplemented by the following historical information based on past classroom experience when students' access to the simulation has been limited to three hours:

- more than 5000: excellent
- 4000 to 5000: very good
- 3000 to 4000: good
- 2000 to 3000: satisfactory
- under 2000: unsatisfactory

With unlimited time, all students should be expected to reach a Share Price Index in excess of 5000. In that case, the discriminating factor is the quality of their report and their understanding of the strategic issues. The decisions and key results of an "Excellent Result" are included as Exhibit D for reference. The Share Price Index attained by this group is 6909 at the end of Period 10. The strategy of this group can be summarized as follows:

- Cut all investments on Trigols and allocate marketing resources *50–50* between Ovadols and Squazols;

- For a given product category in a given period, allocate marketing resources between countries proportionate to market size;

- For Ovadols, spend 40% of the marketing expenditures on Consumer Marketing, the rest on Trade Marketing. For Squazols, this percentage is 70%;

- Identify for each product category and each country the price level which approximately optimizes contribution. This leads to global average prices of 274 for Ovadols (from 320 in Period 0, minus 22%), of 118 for Squazols (from 131, minus 11%), and of 167 for Trigols (from 202, a 24% reduction). The international variation between the lowest and the highest prices was about 30% for all three products;

- Identify the level of local adaptation required to approximately optimize contribution, given the other decisions. This leads to a product adaptation of 40 for Ovadols (down from 90, hence a greater standardization) and zero for Squazols and Trigols (hence total standardization). For all three product categories, adaptation was set at 100 for Consumer Marketing (total local adaptation) and at 50 for Trade Marketing.

This strategy can be improved upon. It has, however, the advantage of being clear and consistent, of exploiting the analysis of the case, and of providing satisfactory results! This is in many ways more rewarding than good results achieved in part through nondocumented, random decisions. The instructor can use it as a reference to develop his or her own plan, test it with the simulation, generate results, and present selected graphs for discussion in class. The registered record at the time of publication of these notes is a share price index of 7520, an improvement of 611 on the above, but with a more complex set of decisions.

Have your students win a new marketing software tool!

If a student in your class has obtained a result which you believe may be a record (for any of the four difficulty levels), please encourage him or her to send a short statement of his/her strategy, as well as a diskette containing the corresponding .dat and .hdr files to:

Mr. Re'mi Triolet
Strat*X
10 Passage de l'Arche, Cedex 62
92056 Paris - La Defense
FRANCE

The five students obtaining the best results (i.e., highest share price index in Period 10) over the past year will receive a marketing software tool from Strat*X. In case of identical results, the five winners will be selected by the authors on the basis of the quality of the strategic statement.

2. *How did you do it?*

The best approach is first to ask the students with the "best" achievement (highest share price index) to present their strategy. This can then be contrasted with the strategies of students with weaker results. Key discussion points are:

- The allocation of resources between product categories. Has anybody withdrawn from at least one category? Did anybody calculate the amount spent on marketing relative to market size or product sales? Contrast the product priority ordering selected for different strategies;

- The allocation of resources between countries. Has anybody decided to withdraw from a given country? Did anybody calculate the amount spent on marketing relative to country market size or country sales? Contrast the country priority ordering selected for different strategies;

- The allocation of resources between consumer and trade marketing. Was this an explicit decision or were independent decisions made for each of the two marketing instruments? Did this ratio vary by product category or by country? What was the rationale for these differences?

- The pricing strategy. How did you determine prices? Did you try to optimize short term CBM in setting price or did you have other objectives? Did you notice changes in the price elasticity of a given product when consumer marketing expenditures varied?

- Global standardization versus local adaptation. Did you have a different approach on this issue for different product categories? Did you make different choices for product specifications, consumer marketing, and trade marketing?

One likely question (or one which should be asked by the instructor) is: "Can the high levels of share price achieved by the best groups be the result of a short term milking strategy which could be detrimental to the long term position of the firm?" This is likely to prompt an interesting debate in which market share will come up as an alternative measure of long term position. At this point, it is valuable to ask each group to state their global market shares per product category in Period 10 and to write them on the board next to their share price index. One can then compare the results of these alternative criteria and raise the broader question: "If you could buy one of these firms, which one would you prefer to buy?" or "Which firm is better positioned for the future?" It is not possible for a CALGOLIA firm to obtain a dramatic increase in its share price through short term milking mechanisms. The computation of the share price corresponds to a projection of future profits *based on the CAM of the last three periods*. In this sense, the stock market evaluation not only considers current profiles, but includes an anticipation for future profits in line with the position of the firm in the last three years. This does not guarantee, however, that the stock market correctly anticipates either the future evolution of market and competitive conditions or the ability of management to tackle future challenges!

3. *What have we learned?*

This question should be asked on the basis of the students' personal experience during the assignment and the class discussion. There are two sets of key lessons. Some are more directly linked to basic issues of Marketing Management. They are related to the textbook and particularly relevant for university students:

- *Marketing mix elasticities.* In a given situation, changes in the various elements of the marketing mix will have a different impact on sales and profits. Marketing research and experimentation help in identifying the levels which maximize long term profits;
- *Marketing mix interactions.* The market reaction to one element of the marketing mix is not independent of other marketing tools. In the GAMAR3 situation, higher levels of consumer marketing reduce the sensitivity of demand to price (and therefore increase the optimum price), within limits;
- *Marketing mix and product life cycle.* The sensitivity of sales and profits to elements of the marketing mix is expected to vary along the product life cycle. In GAMAR3 the elasticity of trade marketing tends to be higher, and the elasticity of consumer marketing lower, for more mature product categories;
- *Marketing analysis.* Systematic analysis is essential for effective decision making in marketing, and it should include both external and internal considerations. In GAMAR3, market information is contained in the Survey and Product sections of the

Company Report. The measures of Consumer Satisfaction and Marketing Effectiveness are essential to understand the impact of the marketing program and to improve it. The Product section provides information on market size, market shares, market prices, and growth projections. The Finance section includes data on product costs and on the profitability structure of the firm;

- *Marketing strategy.* Ultimately, marketing strategy is concerned with allocating resources. In GAMAR3, they must be allocated at three levels—among elements of the marketing mix (consumer and trade marketing), among product categories, and among countries. Clear guidelines must be formulated based on analysis. In the absence of such guidelines, decisions become complex, inconsistent, and ineffective;

- *Marketing monitoring and control.* The nature of marketing is dynamic. Marketing is about change in the market place, coping with it and creating it. It is difficult to bring to life this dynamic perspective in a case discussion. In a simulation like GAMAR3, the succession of decisions and feedback over 10 periods provides the opportunity to observe the dynamics of marketing, and requires continuous monitoring and control.

Other lessons include more general points of marketing strategy and leadership better appreciated by executives, such as:

- *Marketing strategy and learning processes.* Marketing strategy formulation should be based on sound analysis. On the other hand, very seldom will analysis alone provide the definitive marketing strategy which will drive the business for years to come. The process by which marketing strategy is formulated is based on a combination of analysis, discussion, confrontation, experimentation, and feedback. Continuous learning processes are therefore essential for developing and nurturing robust marketing strategies over the long term;

- *Actual strategy formulation is painful.* It is easy to talk about strategy, it is more difficult to reach a consensus on a course of action. This requires making hard choices and ruling out some alternatives. It is already difficult to accept making such choices at the individual level, but if the assignment is given to groups, strategy formulation will usually generate even greater difficulties which have to be resolved through some form of leadership. The group setting provides a context in which constructive conflicts can help the strategy formulation process but the selection of a strategy requires a resolution of these conflicts;

- *Strategy is ultimately concerned with the allocation of resources.* Strategy is only an intellectual statement until it is translated into actual resource allocation decisions. Some assignments will probably illustrate resource allocation decisions that are not consistent with a neatly packaged strategy statement. In this case, the real strategy is not the statement, it is the set of principles underlying the actual decisions, even if this set of principles has not been made explicit.

- *Management time is a key resource.* Managers usually concentrate on the allocation of financial or other tangible resources. GAMAR3 demonstrates to participants that their own time is a crucial resource. Poor products, too many products, lack of strategy, or lack of defined processes result in a dispersion of this crucial resource.

- *Strategy and flexibility.* Strategy provides a general direction for the evolution of the firm. It involves choices, and results in a certain rigidity in the options available for the future. One has to make sure that a certain level of flexibility is left within the general direction set by a given strategy (for instance pricing and marketing investments adjusted in the short term according to specific budgetary constraints).

- *Global standardization versus local adaptation.* The debate between these two extreme approaches to international marketing can sometimes be likened to a religious war. There is in fact no perfect solution combining the positive aspects of both. However, the worst alternative is skirting the issue—the absence of a clear international strategy will lead to widespread inefficiencies. In the end, the degree of local adaptation will have to take into account consumer needs, cost efficiencies, and the value of organizational simplicity.

- *An "optimum" long term strategy is not a succession of "optimum" short term decisions.* It is likely that at least some participants will try to "optimize" their decisions for each period by rerunning the simulation up to 10 times per period. It is easy to demonstrate in the GAMAR3 context that a successful long term strategy may require accepting less than "optimum" short term decisions. One may have to accept lower short term profits to build a stronger market share position—experimentation and learning are essential for good long term results, even if they require making investments and taking risks in the short run.

The instructor may want to emphasize different learning points from the above two sets, depending on the audience and the objective of the CALGOLIA exercise in the context of a given course. Generally, however, the strength of the exercise is that it illustrates concepts related to the dynamics of marketing management and marketing strategy. It is an effective learning tool which is complementary to traditional lectures and cases.

THE GAMAR3 SIMULATION

The GAMAR3 simulation runs on standard 486/Pentium compatible personal computers operating under the Microsoft Windows 3.1 or Windows 95 environment. It requires no special equipment other than a color monitor and a printer. One megabyte of hard disk space is necessary to install the software and to save decisions and results for a full 10-period run of the simulation. Each additional run for a different simulated firm uses 130K bytes of hard disk space.

No computer expertise is needed to operate the simulation. Appendix A of the case gives basic instructions. The Help facility, which provides more detailed operating guidelines, is accessible either directly for the current screen or through the usual Contents and Search options available under Windows.

Students can create firms which they will manage for 10 periods. When they create a firm, they are asked to give it a name of no more than eight characters, including only letters and numbers. If the students have to submit a printed report of the results, it is advisable to assign a different firm name to each participant (or group) in order to avoid confusion. This may simply be the student's own name (e.g., MSMITH) or a group number (e.g., TEAM12). When creating a simulated firm, they also are asked to select a difficulty level. While they can use lower levels of difficulty for practice purposes, the instructor should tell them the level selected for the assignment.

If students use publicly available microcomputers, others can access their GAMAR3 decisions and results. To prevent this from happening, students should save their data files on a floppy disk *and* erase them from the hard disk. In that case they need extra information on the structure of data files. Every time a firm is created, two data files are opened on the hard disk; their name is composed of the name of the corresponding firm followed by the suffix ".dat" for one and ".hdr" for the other. For instance, when the firm "MSMITH" is created, two data files named "MSMITH.DAT" and "MSMITH.HDR" are opened on the hard disk. One should *not rename* GAMAR3 data files, since different names for a simulated firm and the corresponding data files are likely to result in confusion and errors.

The GAMAR3 software allows students to run the simulation for a given period, analyze the results, and rerun the simulation for the same period. In this way they can test different courses of action for a given period, up to 10 test runs per period. But they cannot rerun previous periods. For instance, in Period 6, "GROUP12" can make decisions for the next period, and then either run the simulation for Period 7, or change the decisions for Period 6 and rerun it. But they cannot change the decisions for Periods 1 to 5.

If the students think they have made a serious mistake in an earlier period which they want to correct, their only option is to create a new simulated firm, to reenter decisions, and then to rerun the simulation from Period 1. In the above example, if the members of "GROUP12" want to make a correction in Period 4, they would have to create a new firm, "GROUP12A." They would then run the simulation for "GROUP12A" with the same decisions for Periods 1–3, make the corrections for Period 4, and proceed with the following periods. This approach, which allows students to rerun the current period easily while making corrections of earlier periods possible but more difficult, provides the possibility of testing while preventing what would be purely a "fishing expedition" approach to strategy formulation.

Finally, a microcomputer with projection facilities in the classroom would enable the instructor to demonstrate use of the software in the introductory session and to present results in the concluding session.

Exhibit B

CALGOLIA IN UNDERGRADUATE OR GRADUATE COURSES

CALGOLIA's flexible design makes it possible to use it in many different ways as part of a course on Marketing Principles, Marketing Management, Marketing Strategy, or International Marketing. We will discuss here some key issues concerning the course design, present some typical alternatives, and discuss the possibility of using CALGOLIA as a team project.

1.   KEY ISSUES IN USING THE CALGOLIA PACKAGE IN A COURSE

There are four main questions in deciding on how to incorporate it into a course:

A. How many sessions should be devoted to CALGOLIA?

The number can vary from one to three. Various alternatives according to the number of sessions available are presented below. The three-session alternative makes the best use of the case and simulation and gives students the full benefits of the exercise. The final choice will, however, depend on time constraints, the availability of microcomputers and the instructor's attitude towards computer simulations.

B. Where in the course should CALGOLIA be used?

The best use of CALGOLIA is as an integrative tool towards the end of the course. Before the exercise, students should have a broad perspective on the role of marketing, market behavior, industry dynamics, marketing strategy, and the marketing mix as covered in the Boyd/Walker/ Larréché textbook. The international dimension is present in every chapter of the book and students will have acquired a more global perspective that will also help them to deal better with the CALGOLIA simulation. If students raise issues not directly addressed by the simulation, such as consumer behavior, segmentation, or positioning, the instructor can use this as an opportunity to illustrate the market's sensitivity to alternate elements of the marketing mix.

The concluding session on CALGOLIA can either be the final session of the course or it can take place before addressing the broader issues of Implementation and Control.

Finally, it is best not to spread the CALGOLIA assignment over more than two or three weeks in order not to lose the momentum of such an exercise.

C. Individual assignments or team work?

The CALGOLIA case can be assigned individually or to teams of three to six students. This must be decided by the instructor, taking into account the availability of microcomputers, the requirements of individual grading, and the attitude of the school toward group work. From a strictly pedagogical point of view, team assignments on strategic issues such as those addressed in CALGOLIA force confrontation and debates which enrich the learning process. The team approach should consequently be favored whenever possible.

D. Should there be a time limit?

The GAMAR3 simulation requires two to five hours of work for discussion and to run the simulation on a microcomputer, not including the writing of a report. *If a time limit is set* (two to five hours), for instance in the context of a supervised session in a computer laboratory, results will vary widely according to teams' ability to analyze data, formulate strategies, and test them under time pressure. The class discussion that follows can use these as a starting point. Grading should also be based on the results. *Without a time limit,* there will be much less difference between the results of different teams as they will usually persevere until they reach satisfactory results. The class discussion should then focus on the process of strategy formulation. In this context, it is desirable to ask students to submit a report describing their analysis, their strategy, their experience in implementing it, and the main lessons they have learned. The report can be limited—from three to ten pages (plus exhibits)—according to the importance which the instructor wants to give the exercise. Grading should reflect more the quality of the report than the results obtained.

2. TYPICAL CLASS SCHEDULING ALTERNATIVES

A. Three sessions:

- One session on discussion of the CALGOLIA case (see "Teaching the Introductory Session").
- Student assignment on the simulation for Periods 1 to 5 only.
- One session on student presentations and discussion of the assignment for Periods 1 to 5.
- Student assignment on the simulation for Periods 1 to 10.

- One session on student presentations of their assignment, discussion, and conclusion (see "Teaching the Concluding Session").

B. Two sessions:

- One session on discussion of the CALGOLIA case (see "Teaching the Introductory Session").
- Student assignment on the simulation for Periods 1 to 10.
- One session on student presentations of their assignment, discussion, and conclusions (see "Teaching the Concluding Session").

C. One session only: Debriefing after the CALGOLIA assignment.

The case and simulation are given as a single assignment and the session is devoted to analyzing and discussing the results in the same way as when CALGOLIA is used as a team project (see appropriate section of this Instructor's Manual).

D. One session only: CALGOLIA case as an introduction to the simulation.

Discussion of the case in one session followed by an assignment on the simulation submitted to the instructor one week later without a debriefing session (see "Teaching the Introductory Session" in this Instructor's Manual).

E. One session: CALGOLIA case only.

Discussion of the case without the use of the simulation. This is appropriate only when it is not feasible for all students in the class to have access to microcomputers or when the instructor does not see fit to use computer exercises in the course (see "Teaching the Introductory Session").

3. CALGOLIA AS A TEAM PROJECT

The most unobtrusive way to use the CALGOLIA exercise is as a team project in the second half of a course. Before students embark on this exercise, they should have acquired at least a broad perspective on the role of marketing, market behavior, and industry dynamics. Students should be given one to two weeks to complete the assignment, possibly in groups of three to six. They should be asked to turn in a report presenting their analysis, their strategy, their results, and what they learned from the exercise. It is advisable to limit the size of the report to 10 pages plus exhibits.

The CALGOLIA exercise used as an integrated team project towards the end of a course gives students an opportunity to review and experiment with many concepts such as marketing mix; market evaluation; industry dynamics; portfolio strategy; strategy in growing, mature, and declining markets; decision support systems; international marketing; marketing implementation; and control. In this context, there is no limit on the time students should spend using the simulation and improving their results. All teams are expected to learn in the process and to achieve reasonable results. There will consequently be less differentiation between the performance of the various teams in terms of the Share Price Index than in a situation where time is limited. In this case, the instructor should clearly state at the beginning of the assignment that the emphasis will be on the *quality of the report*. This should be reflected in grading (80% on the report quality and 20% on the results is a good balance).

Although this is not compulsory, it is a good idea to allocate a class session to the CALGOLIA exercise soon after the date at which the reports are due. This session can be organized as follows:

1. **Team presentations:** Fifteen minutes each. Select the number of teams making a presentation according to the time available. Choose the teams for the quality of their reports and for purposes of illustrating different approaches.

2. **Class discussion:** Prompt a discussion on the contrast between the strategies of the different groups; give those who did not make a presentation an opportunity to share their experience.

3. **Conclusion:** Summarize the key learning points from the exercise.

The sections in this teaching note dealing with "Teaching the Introductory Session" and "Teaching the Concluding Session" give more details on the content of class discussion and on concluding learning points.

Exhibit C

CALGOLIA IN EXECUTIVE SEMINARS

Many of the considerations on using CALGOLIA in undergraduate and graduate courses are also relevant for executive seminars. In such a situation, however, there is usually not enough time available to ask executives to write reports, nor is grading a relevant issue. On the other hand, one may have more scheduling flexibility in the case of a residential program. Two schedules are given at the end of this section for executive programs where a half-day or a full day are devoted to CALGOLIA.

Allocating two hours to group work is a bare minimum and puts the executives under severe pressure. CALGOLIA has been used many times in this fashion with great success, but it requires very good handling.

The instructor should first make sure that by the end of the introductory session, the executives have a good understanding of the issues in CALGOLIA. He or she should also check that at least one person in each group is familiar with the basic operation of a PC under MS Windows or Windows 95. Computer assistance should be provided, with an assistant ready to intervene—in case the printer jams, for example. The instructor must also make sure that the executives do not get stuck in the group discussion. He or she should point out that, if there is a deep disagreement on the best course of action, it is easier to simulate several test runs for a given period than to try to argue it out.

If the schedule allows more than a half-day for the CALGOLIA exercise, it will prove both more valuable to the executives and easier to run. Depending on the time available, priority improvements on the suggested schedule would be: (1) more time for group work; (2) a longer final session; (3) a longer introductory session; and/or (4) adding an intermediate review session. The full-day schedule below implements several of these options.

1. Half-day version of executive CALGOLIA schedule

Previous evening: participants should familiarize themselves with the CALGOLIA case.

08:30 - 9:45: Session 1: Introduction

> Case Discussion
> Demonstration of the GAMAR3 software

10:00 - 12:00: Group Work

> Preparation of strategic plan
> Testing and finalizing; using the simulation

12:00 - 12:30: Session 2: Conclusions

> Group presentation of results
> Discussion
> Conclusion: learning points

2. Full-day version of executive CALGOLIA schedule

Previous evening: participants should familiarize themselves with the CALGOLIA case.

08:30 - 10:00: Session 1: Introduction

> Case Discussion
> Demonstration of GAMAR3 software

10:15 - 12:30: Group Work

    Preparation of strategic plan for Periods 1 to 10
    Testing and update of plan for Periods 1 to 5, using the simulation

12:30 - 13:30: Lunch

13:30 - 14:00: Session 2: Intermediate review session

    Debriefing of intermediate results
    Conclusions on key selected learning points

14:00 - 16:00 Group Work

    Revision of strategic plan for Periods 1 to 10
    Testing and finalizing of plan for Periods 1 to 10, using the simulation

16:15 - 17:15 Session 3: Conclusions

    Group presentation of results
    Discussion
    Conclusion: learning points

Exhibit D: Example of an "Excellent" GAMAR3 Plan—Period 1

Product Category	Country	Management Time (man-months)	Consumer Marketing (K$)	Trade Marketing (K$)	Price ($)	Local Adaptations (0 = none – 100 = total) Product Specs	Consumer Marketing	Trade Marketing
OVADOLS	U-K	21	3600	1900	240.00			
	Poland	36	1400	1000	312.00			
	France	21	1900	1000	255.00	50	50	50
	Germany	21	2500	1500	265.00			
	Italy	21	2200	1500	300.00			
SQUAZOLS	U-K	28	2700	1600	100.00			
	Poland	28	1350	800	130.00			
	France	28	1600	1000	105.00	50	50	50
	Germany	28	2200	1300	125.00			
	Italy	28	1600	900	130.00			
TRIGOLS	U-K	20	2200	1100	150.00			
	Poland	20	1100	550	195.00			
	France	20	1200	550	165.00	50	50	50
	Germany	20	1600	800	160.00			
	Italy	20	1500	700	165.00			

Country Specific Decisions

121

Exhibit D: Example of an "Excellent" GAMAR3 Plan—Period 2

Product Category	Country	Country Specific Decisions				Local Adaptations (0 = none – 100 = total)		
		Management Time (man-months)	Consumer Marketing (K$)	Trade Marketing (K$)	Price ($)	Product Specs	Consumer Marketing	Trade Marketing
OVADOLS	U-K	21	3600	3600	240.00			
	Poland	36	1800	1800	312.00			
	France	21	1900	1900	255.00	50	50	50
	Germany	21	3000	3000	265.00			
	Italy	21	2400	2400	300.00			
SQUAZOLS	U-K	28	3600	3600	100.00			
	Poland	28	1800	1800	130.00			
	France	28	1900	1900	105.00	50	50	50
	Germany	28	3000	3000	125.00			
	Italy	28	2400	2400	130.00			
TRIGOLS	U-K	20	1000	1300	150.00			
	Poland	20	700	700	195.00			
	France	20	700	700	165.00	50	50	50
	Germany	20	900	900	160.00			
	Italy	20	800	800	165.00			

122

Exhibit D: Example of an "Excellent" GAMAR3 Plan—Period 3

Product Category	Country Specific Decisions					Local Adaptations (0 = none – 100 = total)		
	Country	Management Time (man-months)	Consumer Marketing (K$)	Trade Marketing (K$)	Price ($)	Product Specs	Consumer Marketing	Trade Marketing
OVADOLS	U-K	36	5000	6100	240.00			
	Poland	36	2400	3000	312.00			
	France	36	2600	3200	255.00	50	50	50
	Germany	36	4100	5100	265.00			
	Italy	36	3300	4100	300.00			
SQUAZOLS	U-K	36	6300	4200	100.00			
	Poland	36	3700	2400	130.00			
	France	36	3900	2600	105.00	50	50	50
	Germany	36	5600	3700	125.00			
	Italy	36	4000	2600	130.00			
TRIGOLS	U-K	0	0	0	150.00			
	Poland	0	0	0	195.00			
	France	0	0	0	165.00	50	50	50
	Germany	0	0	0	160.00			
	Italy	0	0	0	165.00			

Exhibit D: Example of an "Excellent" GAMAR3 Plan—Period 4

Product Category	Country	Country Specific Decisions					Local Adaptations (0 = none – 100 = total)		
		Management Time (man-months)	Consumer Marketing (K$)	Trade Marketing (K$)	Price ($)		Product Specs	Consumer Marketing	Trade Marketing
OVADOLS	U-K	36	6700	8200	240.00		40	100	50
	Poland	36	3600	4400	312.00				
	France	36	3900	4700	255.00				
	Germany	36	6100	7500	265.00				
	Italy	36	4800	5900	300.00				
SQUAZOLS	U-K	36	8600	5700	100.00		0	100	50
	Poland	36	5300	3500	130.00				
	France	36	5400	3600	105.00				
	Germany	36	8400	5600	125.00				
	Italy	36	5700	3800	130.00				
TRIGOLS	U-K	0	0	0	150.00		0	0	0
	Poland	0	0	0	195.00				
	France	0	0	0	165.00				
	Germany	0	0	0	160.00				
	Italy	0	0	0	165.00				

Exhibit D: Example of an "Excellent" GAMAR3 Plan—Period 5

Product Category	Country	Country Specific Decisions				Local Adaptations (0 = none – 100 = total)		
		Management Time (man-months)	Consumer Marketing (K$)	Trade Marketing (K$)	Price ($)	Product Specs	Consumer Marketing	Trade Marketing
OVADOLS	U-K	36	7200	10600	240.00			
	Poland	36	3700	7900	312.00			
	France	36	5100	6000	255.00	40	100	50
	Germany	36	6300	11200	265.00			
	Italy	36	6200	7300	300.00			
SQUAZOLS	U-K	36	12000	5300	100.00			
	Poland	36	7300	4900	130.00			
	France	36	10600	3500	105.00	0	100	50
	Germany	36	11300	5300	125.00			
	Italy	36	11300	3500	130.00			
TRIGOLS	U-K	0	0	0	150.00			
	Poland	0	0	0	195.00			
	France	0	0	0	165.00	0	0	0
	Germany	0	0	0	160.00			
	Italy	0	0	0	165.00			

125

Exhibit D: Example of an "Excellent" GAMAR3 Plan—Period 6

Product Category	Country	Management Time (man-months)	Consumer Marketing (K$)	Trade Marketing (K$)	Price ($)	Product Specs	Consumer Marketing	Trade Marketing
						Local Adaptations (0 = none – 100 = total)		
OVADOLS	U-K	36	7500	11000	240.00			
	Poland	36	4000	8300	312.00			
	France	36	5400	6400	255.00	40	100	50
	Germany	36	6600	11600	265.00			
	Italy	36	6500	7700	300.00			
SQUAZOLS	U-K	36	12000	5300	100.00			
	Poland	36	7300	4900	130.00			
	France	36	10600	3500	105.00	0	100	50
	Germany	36	11300	5300	125.00			
	Italy	36	11300	3500	130.00			
TRIGOLS	U-K	0	0	0	150.00			
	Poland	0	0	0	195.00			
	France	0	0	0	165.00	0	0	0
	Germany	0	0	0	160.00			
	Italy	0	0	0	165.00			

Exhibit D: Example of an "Excellent" GAMAR3 Plan—Period 7

| Product Category | Country | Country Specific Decisions | | | | | Local Adaptations (0 = none – 100 = total) | | |
		Management Time (man-months)	Consumer Marketing (K$)	Trade Marketing (K$)	Price ($)	Product Specs	Consumer Marketing	Trade Marketing
OVADOLS	U-K	36	7500	11000	240.00			
	Poland	36	4000	8300	312.00			
	France	36	5400	6400	255.00	40	100	50
	Germany	36	6600	11600	265.00			
	Italy	36	6500	7700	300.00			
SQUAZOLS	U-K	36	12000	5300	100.00			
	Poland	36	7300	4900	130.00			
	France	36	10600	3500	105.00	0	100	50
	Germany	36	11300	5300	125.00			
	Italy	36	11300	3500	130.00			
TRIGOLS	U-K	0	0	0	150.00			
	Poland	0	0	0	195.00			
	France	0	0	0	165.00	0	0	0
	Germany	0	0	0	160.00			
	Italy	0	0	0	165.00			

127

Exhibit D: Example of an "Excellent" GAMAR3 Plan—Period 8

Product Category	Country Specific Decisions					Local Adaptations (0 = none – 100 = total)		
	Country	Management Time (man-months)	Consumer Marketing (K$)	Trade Marketing (K$)	Price ($)	Product Specs	Consumer Marketing	Trade Marketing
OVADOLS	U-K	36	7500	11000	240.00	40	100	50
	Poland	36	4000	8300	312.00			
	France	36	5400	6400	255.00			
	Germany	36	6600	11600	265.00			
	Italy	36	6500	7700	300.00			
SQUAZOLS	U-K	36	12000	5300	100.00	0	100	50
	Poland	36	7300	4900	130.00			
	France	36	10600	3500	105.00			
	Germany	36	11300	5300	125.00			
	Italy	36	11300	3500	130.00			
TRIGOLS	U-K	0	0	0	150.00	0	0	0
	Poland	0	0	0	195.00			
	France	0	0	0	165.00			
	Germany	0	0	0	160.00			
	Italy	0	0	0	165.00			

Exhibit D: Example of an "Excellent" GAMAR3 Plan—Period 9

Product Category	Country	Country Specific Decisions				Local Adaptations (0 = none – 100 = total)		
		Management Time (man-months)	Consumer Marketing (K$)	Trade Marketing (K$)	Price ($)	Product Specs	Consumer Marketing	Trade Marketing
OVADOLS	U-K	36	7500	11000	240.00	40	100	50
	Poland	36	4000	8300	312.00			
	France	36	5400	6400	255.00			
	Germany	36	6600	11600	265.00			
	Italy	36	6500	7700	300.00			
SQUAZOLS	U-K	36	12000	5300	100.00	0	100	50
	Poland	36	7300	4900	130.00			
	France	36	10600	3500	105.00			
	Germany	36	11300	5300	125.00			
	Italy	36	11300	3500	130.00			
TRIGOLS	U-K	0	0	0	150.00	0	0	0
	Poland	0	0	0	195.00			
	France	0	0	0	165.00			
	Germany	0	0	0	160.00			
	Italy	0	0	0	165.00			

Exhibit D: Example of an "Excellent" GAMAR3 Plan—Period 10

| Product Category | Country | Country Specific Decisions | | | | | Local Adaptations (0 = none – 100 = total) | | |
		Management Time (man-months)	Consumer Marketing (K$)	Trade Marketing (K$)	Price ($)	Product Specs	Consumer Marketing	Trade Marketing
OVADOLS	U-K	36	7500	11000	240.00			
	Poland	36	4000	8300	312.00			
	France	36	5400	6400	255.00	40	100	50
	Germany	36	6600	11600	265.00			
	Italy	36	6500	7700	300.00			
SQUAZOLS	U-K	36	12000	5300	100.00			
	Poland	36	7300	4900	130.00			
	France	36	10600	3500	105.00	0	100	50
	Germany	36	11300	5300	125.00			
	Italy	36	11300	3500	130.00			
TRIGOLS	U-K	0	0	0	150.00			
	Poland	0	0	0	195.00			
	France	0	0	0	165.00	0	0	0
	Germany	0	0	0	160.00			
	Italy	0	0	0	165.00			

130

TRANSPARENCY MASTERS

Chapter	Transparency Number and Identification	
10	TM10-3	Marketing Actions to Achieve Share-Maintenance Objectives
	TM10-4	Strategic Choices for Share Leaders in Growth Markets
	TM10-5	Marketing Objectives of Share-Maintenance Strategies in Growth Markets
	TM10-6	Marketing Actions to Achieve Share-Growth Objectives
	TM10-7	Strategic Choices for Challengers in Growth Markets
	TM10-8	Marketing Objectives of Share-Growth Strategies
	TM10-9	Strategic Changes Made by Challengers That Gained or Lost Market Share
11	TM11-1	The Transition or Shakeout Stage of the Generalized Product Life Cycle
	TM11-2	Three Strategic Disciplines of Market Leaders and the Traits of Businesses That Implement Them Effectively
	TM11-3	Dimensions of Product Quality
	TM11-4	Dimensions of Service Quality
	TM11-5	Perceived Importance of Service Quality Dimensions in Four Different Industries
	TM11-6	Determinants of Perceived Service Quality
	TM11-7	Sources of Increased Profit From Loyal Customers
	TM11-8	Factors Affecting the Attractiveness of Declining Markets
12	TM12-1	Administrative Factors Related to the Successful Implementation of Business Strategies
	TM12-2	Organizational and Interfunctional Factors Related to the Successful Implementation of Business Strategies
	TM12-3	A Marketing Department with a Product Management Organization
	TM12-4	Contents of an Annual Marketing Plan
13	TM13-1	The Control Process
	TM13-2	Finding Product or Entry Profitability with Full Costing and Marginal Contribution Methods (in $000s)

TM 1-1 Exhibit 1–1
The Hierarchy of Strategies

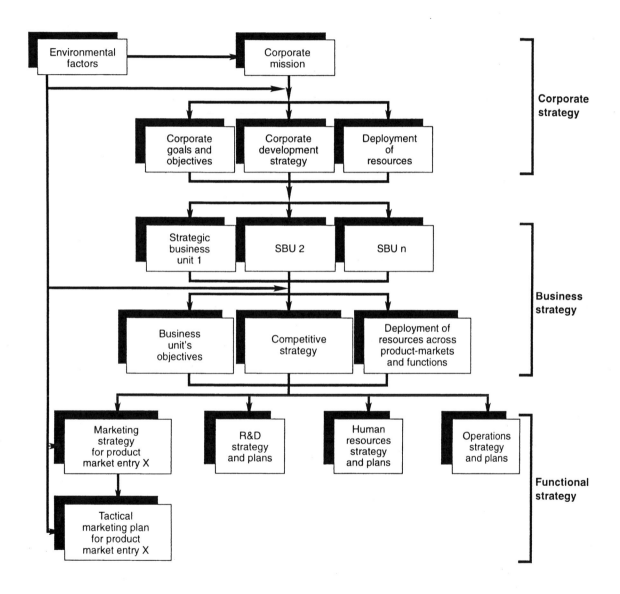

Strategy components	Corporate strategy	Business strategy	Marketing strategy
Scope	• Corporate domain—"Which businesses should we be in?" • Corporate development strategy Conglomerate diversification (expansion into unrelated businesses) Vertical integration Acquisition and divestiture policies	• Business domain—"Which product-markets should we be in within this business or industry?" • Business development strategy Concentric diversification (new products for existing customers or new customers for existing products)	• Target market definition • Product-line depth and breadth • Branding policies • Product-market development plan • Line extension and product elimination plans
Goals and objectives	• Overall corporate objectives aggregated across businesses Revenue growth Profitability ROI (return on investment) Earnings per share Contributions to other stakeholders	• Constrained by corporate goals • Objectives aggregated across product-market entries in the business unit Sales growth New product or market growth Profitability ROI Cash flow Strengthening bases of competitive advantage	• Constrained by corporate and business goals • Objectives for a specific product-market entry Sales Market share Contribution margin Customer satisfaction
Allocation of resources	• Allocation among businesses in the corporate portfolio • Allocation across functions shared by multiple businesses (corporate R&D, MIS)	• Allocation among product-market entries in the business unit • Allocation across functional departments within the business unit	• Allocation across components of the marketing plan (elements of the marketing mix) for a specific product-market entry
Sources of competitive advantage	• Primarily through superior corporate financial or human resources; more corporate R&D; better organizational processes or synergies relative to competitors across all industries in which the firm operates	• Primarily through competitive strategy; business unit's competencies relative to competitors in its industry	• Primarily through effective product positioning; superiority on one or more components of the marketing mix relative to competitors within a specific product-market
Sources of synergy	• Shared resources, technologies, or functional competencies across businesses within the firm	• Shared resources (including favorable customer image) or functional competencies across product-markets within an industry	• Shared marketing resources, competencies, or activities across product-market entries

TM 1-3 Exhibit 1-3
Characteristics of Alternative Planning Systems

Type of planning system

Characteristic	Financial planning	Long-range planning	Strategic planning	Strategic management
Management emphasis	Control budget deviations	Anticipate growth and manage complexity	Creative response to changing environment by changing strategic thrust and capabilities	Cope with strategic surprises and fast-developing opportunities or threats
Major assumptions	The past repeats	Past trends will continue	New trends and discontinuities are predictable	Planning cycles are inadequate to deal with rapid changes
Direction of strategic decision making	Top-down	Bottom-up	Mixed (leaning toward top-down)	Mixed (leaning toward bottom-up)
Planning time frame	Periodic	Periodic	Periodic	Real time
Underlying value system	Meet the budget	Predict the future	Think strategically	Create the future
Time period when first developed	Early 1900s	1950s	1960s	Mid-1970s

SOURCE: Adapted from F. Gluck, S. Kaufman, and A. Walleck. "The Four Phases of Strategic Management," *Journal of Business Strategy,* Winter 1982, pp. 9–21; D. Aaker, *Strategic Market Management,* 2nd ed. (New York: John Wiley & Sons, 1988), p. 10; and R. Kerin, V. Mahajan, and P. Varadarajan, *Contemporary Perspectives on Strategic Market Planning* (Boston: Allyn and Bacon, 1990), p. 18.

Irwin/McGraw-Hill

The McGraw-Hill Companies, Inc., 1999

Influence and Participation in Strategic Management by Marketing Managers at General Electric

Strategic planning activity	Marketing's role
Determination of SBU's objectives and scope	Key participant along with SBU's general manager
Environmental assessment (customers; economic, political, regulatory trends)	Primary contributor and a major beneficiary of the results
Competitive assessment (actual and potential competitors)	Primary contributor, working with other functional managers and staff planners
Situation assessment (input to portfolio analysis; industry and market attractiveness; firm and product position)	Primary contributor, working with staff planners and general manager
Objectives and goals	Key participant with other functional managers, including responsibility for measuring several performance indicators
Strategies	Major contributor to determination of SBU's competitive strategy; responsible for marketing strategy and for coordinating plans with other functional strategies
Key program elements	**Marketing's role**
Product-market development	Leadership role
Product quality	Leading responsibility for quality
Distribution	Primary responsibility
Technology	Varies according to the importance of technology to the product or service
Human resources	Responsible for functional area
Business development*	Key supporting role with strategic planning and manufacturing responsible for implementation
Manufacturing facilities	Typically, only limited involvement

*Decisions to expand, improve, or contract the business.

SOURCE: Adapted from a speech presented by Stephen G. Harrell (then of the General Electric Company) at the American Marketing Association Educator's Conference, Chicago, August 5, 1980. Mr. Harrell is currently a Partner in Megamark Partners, a consulting firm specializing in marketing and new product development. Reprinted by permission of the American Marketing Association.

TM 1-5 Exhibit 1–8
The Process of Formulating and Implementing Marketing Strategy

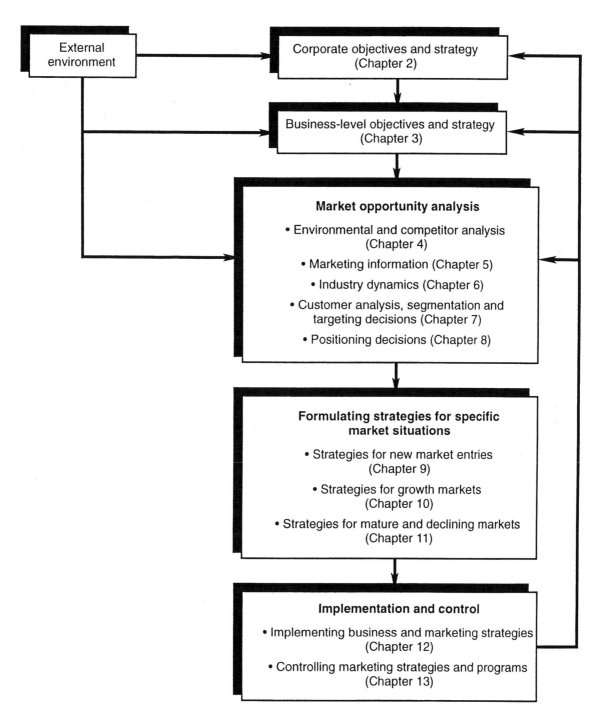

External environment

Corporate objectives and strategy
(Chapter 2)

Business-level objectives and strategy
(Chapter 3)

Market opportunity analysis

• Environmental and competitor analysis
(Chapter 4)

• Marketing information (Chapter 5)

• Industry dynamics (Chapter 6)

• Customer analysis, segmentation and
targeting decisions (Chapter 7)

• Positioning decisions (Chapter 8)

**Formulating strategies for specific
market situations**

• Strategies for new market entries
(Chapter 9)

• Strategies for growth markets
(Chapter 10)

• Strategies for mature and declining markets
(Chapter 11)

Implementation and control

• Implementing business and marketing strategies
(Chapter 12)

• Controlling marketing strategies and programs
(Chapter 13)

TM 2-1 Exhibit 2-1
Corporate Strategy Components and Issues

Strategy component	Key issues
Scope, mission, and intent	• What business(es) should the firm be in? • What customer needs, market segments, and/or technologies should be focused on? • What is the firm's enduring strategic purpose or intent?
Objectives	• What performance dimensions should the firm's business units and employees focus on? • What is the target level of performance to be achieved on each dimension? • What is the time frame in which each target should be attained?
Development strategy	• How can the firm achieve a desired level of growth over time? • Can the desired growth be attained by expanding the firm's current businesses? • Will the company have to diversify into new businesses or product-markets to achieve its future growth objectives?
Resource allocation	• How should the firm's limited financial resources be allocated across its businesses to produce the highest returns? • Of the alternative strategies that each business might pursue, which will produce the greatest returns for the dollars invested?
Sources of synergy	• What competencies, knowledge, and customer-based intangibles (e.g., brand recognition, reputation) might be developed and shared across the firm's businesses? • What operational resources, facilities, or functions (e.g., plants, R&D, salesforce) might the firm's businesses share to increase their efficiency?

Irwin/McGraw-Hill

The Burlington Northern: Characteristics of an Effective Corporate Mission Statement

	Broad	**Specific**
Functional Based on customer needs	Transportation business	Long-distance transportation for large-volume producers of low-value, low-density products
Physical Based on existing products or technology	Railroad business	Long-haul, coal-carrying railroad

SOURCE: Reprinted by permission from p. 43 of *Strategy Formulation: Analytical Concepts* by C. W. Hofer and D. Schendel. Copyright © 1978 by West Publishing Company. All rights reserved.

Irwin/McGraw-Hill

The McGraw-Hill Companies, Inc., 1999

Common Performance Criteria and Measures that Specify Corporate, Business-Unit, and Marketing Objectives

Performance criteria	Possible measures or indexes
• Growth	$ sales Unit sales Percent change in sales
• Competitive strength	Market share Brand awareness Brand preference
• Innovativeness	$ sales from new products Percentage of sales from product-market entries introduced within past five years Percentage cost savings from new processes
• Profitability	$ profits Profit as percentage of sales Contribution margin* Return on investment (ROI) Return on net assets (RONA) Return on equity (ROE)
• Utilization of resources	Percent capacity utilization Fixed assets as percentage of sales
• Contribution to owners	Earnings per share Price/earnings ratio
• Contribution to customers	Price relative to competitors Product quality Customer satisfaction
• Contribution to employees	Wage rates, benefits Personnel development, promotions Employment stability, turnover
• Contribution to society	$ contributions to charities or community institutions Growth in employment

*Business-unit managers and marketing managers responsible for a product-market entry often have little control over costs associated with corporate overhead, such as the costs of corporate staff or R&D. It can be difficult to allocate those costs to specific strategic business units (SBUs) or products. Consequently, profit objectives at the SBU and product-market level are often stated as a desired *contribution margin* (the gross profit prior to allocating such overhead costs).

	Current products	New products

Current markets	**Market penetration strategies**
	• Increase market share
	• Increase product usage
	    Increase frequency of use
	    Increase quantity used
	    New applications
		Product development strategies
		• Product improvements
		• Product-line extensions
		• New products for same market

New markets	**Market development strategies**
	• Expand markets for existing products
	    Geographic expansion
	    Target new segments
		Diversification strategies
		• Vertical integration
		    Forward integration
		    Backward integration
		• Diversification into related businesses (concentric diversification)
		• Diversification into unrelated businesses (conglomerate diversification)

TM 2-5 Exhibit 2–8
BCG's Market Growth–Relative Share Matrix

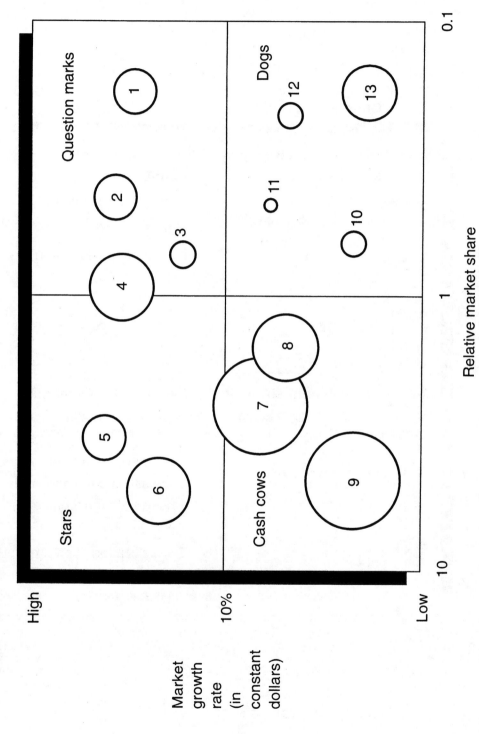

SOURCE: Adapted from Barry Hedley, "Strategy and the Business Portfolio," *Long Range Planning* 10 (February 1977). Reprinted with permission from Elsevier Science.

Irwin/McGraw-Hill

The McGraw-Hill Companies, Inc., 1999

TM 2-6 Exhibit 2–9
Cash Flows across Businesses in the BCG Portfolio Model

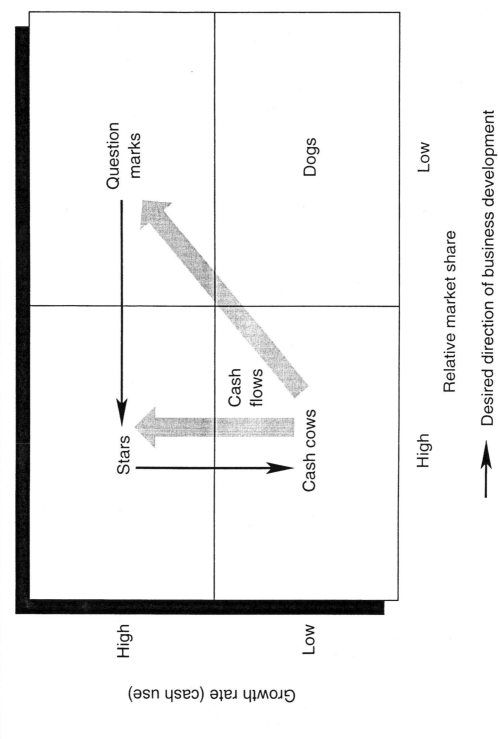

© *The McGraw-Hill Companies, Inc., 1999*

Irwin/McGraw-Hill

TM 2-7 Exhibit 2–10
The Industry Attractiveness-Business Position Matrix

Industry Attractiveness

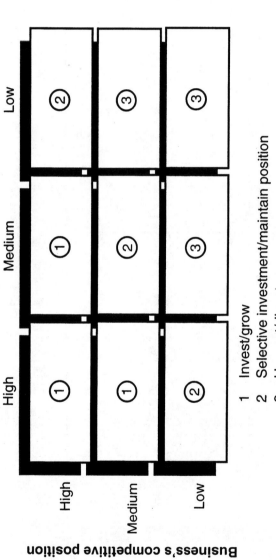

	High	Medium	Low
High	①	①	②
Medium	①	②	③
Low	②	③	③

Business's competitive position

1 Invest/grow
2 Selective investment/maintain position
3 Harvest/divest

Variables that might be used to evaluate:

Business's competitive position

Size
Growth
Relative share
Customer loyalty
Margins

Distribution
Technology
Marketing skills
Patents

Industry attractiveness

Size
Growth
Competitive intensity
Price levels

Profitability
Technological
  sophistication
Government regulations

SOURCE: The Industry Attractiveness-Business Position Matrix.

The McGraw-Hill Companies, Inc., 1999

Irwin/McGraw-Hill

TM 2-8 Exhibit 2–11
Factors Affecting the Creation of Shareholder Value

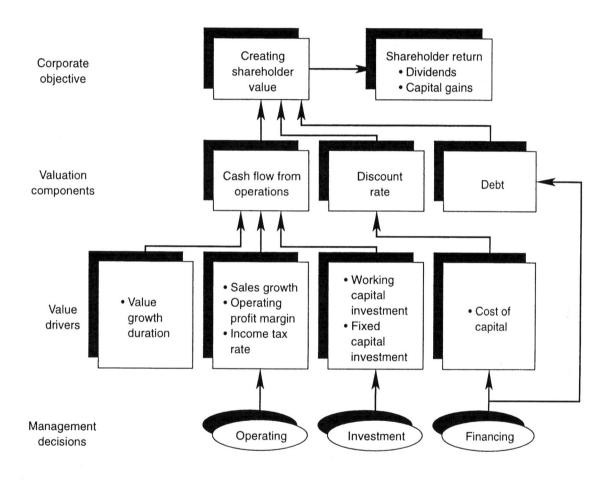

SOURCE: Reprinted with the permission of The Free Press, a Division of Macmillan, Inc., from *Creating Shareholder Value* by Alfred Rappaport. Copyright © 1986 by Alfred Rappaport.

Irwin/McGraw-Hill

The McGraw-Hill Companies, Inc., 1999

TM 3-1 Exhibit 3-2
Porter's Four Business Strategies

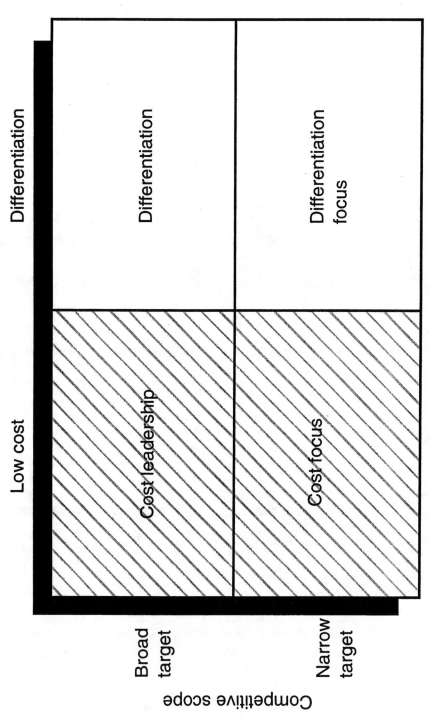

Source of competitive advantage

	Low cost	Differentiation
Broad target	Cost leadership	Differentiation
Narrow target	Cost focus	Differentiation focus

Competitive scope

Source: Adapted with permission of The Free Press, A Division of Macmillan, Inc., from *Competitive Advantage: Creating and Sustaining Superior Performance* by Michael E. Porter. Copyright © 1985 by Michael E. Porter.

TM 3-2 Exhibit 3–4
Combined Typology of Business-Unit Competitive Strategies

Emphasis on new product-market growth

Heavy emphasis ←——————→ No emphasis

	Prospector	Analyzer	Defender	Reactor
Differentiation	Units primarily concerned with attaining growth through aggressive pursuit of new product-market opportunities	Units with strong core business; actively seeking to expand into related product-markets with differentiated offerings	Units primarily concerned with maintaining a **differentiated** position in mature markets	Units with no clearly defined product-market development or competitive strategy
Cost leadership		Units with strong core business; actively seeking to expand into related product-markets with low-cost offerings	Units primarily concerned with maintaining a **low-cost** position in mature markets	

Competitive strategy

Irwin/McGraw-Hill

TM 3-3 Exhibit 3-6
How Business Strategies Differ in Scope, Objectives, Resource Deployments, and Synergy

Dimensions	Low-cost defender	Differentiated defender	Prospector	Analyzer
¥ Scope	Mature/stable/well-defined domain; mature technology and customer segments	Mature/stable/well-defined domain; mature technology and customer segments	Broad/dynamic domains; technology and customer segments not well established	Mixture of defender and prospector strategies
¥ Goals and objectives				
Adaptability (new product success)	Very little	Little	Extensive	Mixture of defender and prospector strategies
Effectiveness (increase in market share)	Little	Little	Large	Mixture of defender and prospector strategies
Efficiency (ROI)	High	High	Low	Mixture of defender and prospector strategies
¥ Resource deployment	Generate excess cash (cash cows)	Generate excess cash (cash cows)	Need cash for product development (question marks or stars)	Need cash for product development but less so than prospectors
¥ Synergy	Need to seek operating synergies to achieve efficiencies	Need to seek operating synergies to achieve efficiencies	Danger in sharing operating facilities and programs better to share technology/marketing skills	Danger in sharing operating facilities and programs better to share technology/marketing skills

Irwin/McGraw-Hill

TM 3-4 Exhibit 3-7
Environmental Factors Favorable to Different Business Strategies

External factors	Prospector	Analyzer	Differentiated defender	Low-cost defender
Market characteristics	• Introductory or early growth stage of industry life cycle • Many unidentified or undeveloped customer segments	• Late growth or early maturity stage of industry life cycle • Some segments well established but potential segments or applications remain undeveloped	• Maturity or decline stage of industry life cycle • Most segments well developed; sales primarily due to repeat/replacement purchases	• Maturity or decline stage of industry life cycle • Most segments well developed; sales primarily due to repeat/replacement purchases
Technology	• Newly emerging technology	• Basic technology well developed but product improvements/modifications still possbile	• Basic technology fully developed and stable	• Basic technology fully developed and stable
Competition	• Few established competitors • Industry structure still emerging	• Many competitors • Industry structure still emerging • Changes in relative market shares likely	• Several well established competitors • Industry structure stable but consolidation is possible	• Several well established competitors • Industry structure stable, but consolidation is possible
Business's relative strengths	• R&D • Product engineering • Marketing research • Marketing/sales	• Process engineering • Efficient production • Marketing/sales • Distributor relations • Customer service	• Process engineering • Quality control • Distributor relations • Marketing/sales • Customer service	• Process engineering • Efficient production • Supplier relations • Distributor relations

The Relationship between Product Quality and Pretax ROI by Business Type

	Quality level				
	Lowest	Below average	Average	Above average	Highest
Consumer durables	16%	18%	18%	26%	32%
Consumer nondurables	15	21	17	23	32
Capital goods	10	8	13	20	21
Raw materials	13	21	21	21	35
Components	12	20	20	22	36
Supplies	16	13	19	25	36

Note: Numbers refer to percent average ROI.

SOURCE: Robert D. Buzzell, "Product Quality," *Pimsletter* no. 4 (Cambridge, Mass.: The Strategic Planning Institute, 1986), p. 5.

Irwin/McGraw-Hill

The McGraw-Hill Companies, Inc., 1999

Differences in Marketing Policies and Program Components across Businesses Pursuing Different Strategies

Marketing policies and program components	Strategy		
	Prospector	Differentiated defender	Low-cost defender
Product policies			
• Product line breadth relative to competitors	+	+	−
• Technical sophistication of products relative to competitors	+	+	−
• Product quality relative to competitors	?	+	−
• Service quality relative to competitors	?	+	−
Price policies			
• Price levels relative to competitors	+	+	−
Distribution policies			
• Degree of forward vertical integration relative to competitors	−	+	?
• Trade promotion expenses as percentage of sales relative to competitors	+	−	−
Promotion policies			
• Advertising expenses as percentage of sales relative to competitors	+	?	−
• Sales promotion expenses as percentage of sales relative to competitors	+	?	−
• Salesforce expenses as percentage of sales relative to competitors	?	+	−

KEY: Plus sign (+) = greater than the average competitor
Minus sign (–) = smaller than the average competitor
Question mark (?) = uncertain relationship between strategy and marketing policy or program component

TM 4-1 Exhibit 4–5
Shifting Values in Western Societies

Traditional values	New values
Self-denial ethic	Self-fulfillment ethic
Higher standard of living	Better quality of life
Traditional sex roles	Blurring of sex roles
Accepted definition of success	Individualized definition of success
Traditional family life	Alternative families
Faith in industry, institutions	Self-reliance
Live to work	Work to live
Hero worship	Love of ideas
Expansionism	Pluralism
Patriotism	Less nationalistic
Unparalleled growth	Growing sense of limits
Industrial growth	Information/service growth
Receptivity to technology	Technology orientation

Developed Western societies are gradually moving away from traditional values and toward the emerging new values being embraced on an ever-widening scale, says author Joseph Plummer.

SOURCE: "Changing Values: The New Emphasis on Self-Actualization," *The Futurist*, January–February 1989, p. 15.

Irwin/McGraw-Hill

The McGraw-Hill Companies, Inc., 1999

Exhibit 4–6
Opportunity/Threat Matrix for a Telecommunications Company

Level of impact on company*	Probability of occurrence (2010)	
	High	Low
High	4	1
Low	2	3

1. Wireless communications technology will make networks based on fiber and copper wires redundant.
2. Technology will provide for the storage and accessing of vast quantities of data at affordable costs.
3. The prices of large-screen (over 36-inch) digitalized TV sets will be reduced by 50 percent (constant dollars).
4. Telephone companies will emerge as the dominant force in the telecommunications industry as well as the operators of telecommunications systems.

*Profits or market share or both.

Irwin/McGraw-Hill

© *The McGraw-Hill Companies, Inc., 1999*

1. **Opposition strategy:** The effectiveness of this strategy is limited because environmental factors are largely beyond the control of a firm. In some situations, a firm may, however, try to delay, attenuate, or otherwise influence an environmental force. Lobbying and corporate issue advertising are examples of opposition strategy used by some large firms.

2. **Adaptation strategy:** Adaptations are often compulsory as, for example, is the case with legislation on product specifications, packaging, and labeling. Choices often exist, however, in the type and extent of adaptation. The danger is that if an adaptation strategy is pursued to the extreme, the environment (not management) sets the pace and scope of strategic change.

3. **Offensive strategy:** Such a strategy uses the environmental issue to improve the firm's competitive position. A key environmental issue may have a destabilizing effect on an industry, which may create opportunities for the more aggressive firms. This was the type of strategy used by Merck in its offer to cut its prices to Medicaid programs. Merck's discounts would be 7 to 13 percent less than the company's regular wholesale prices.

4. **Redeployment strategy:** Faced with major environmental issues in one market, a firm may decide to redeploy its resources in other, less-exposed areas. For example, tobacco companies such as Philip Morris and R. J. Reynolds have diversified into other consumer goods because of the environmental pressures concerning the health effects of cigarette smoking.

5. **Contingency strategies:** One such strategy decreases the risk of being exposed to potentially harmful environmental events. For example, a search may be launched for substitutes for raw materials with volatile prices. Another contingency strategy designs alternative courses of action corresponding to the different possible evolutions of the environment. This involves isolating discrete environmental scenarios the firm may have to face in the future and designing appropriate responses for each. For example, in the early 1990s, gasoline-fueled cars were restricted in certain localities (e.g., Los Angeles) and, thus, some automobile companies began experimenting with electric cars and natural gas-powered vehicles.

6. **Passive strategy:** This strategy calls for not responding to an environmental threat or opportunity. For example, in the early days of modern consumerism, some corporations took major public action to oppose their critics—which only provided greater exposure to the issue and worsened their images. A better alternative would have been not to have taken *any* action until performing more complete analyses and formulating an appropriate response.

TM 5-1 Exhibit 5–4
Steps in the Marketing Research Process and Potential Sources of Errors

Steps	Potential error
1. Problem formulation	Management identifies the wrong problem or defines it poorly.
2. Determining information needs and data sources	Management fails to identify the specific information needed for decision making or the researcher uses the wrong source.
3. Research design, including questionnaire	Ambiguous questions or poor experimental designs result in invalid responses.
4. Sample design and size	Sample procedures result in the selection of a biased sample.
5. Data collection	Errors are caused by nonrespondents, by poor selection of respondents, by the interviewer, or by the nature of interviewer/respondent interaction.
6. Tabulation and analysis	Errors occur while transforming raw data from questionnaires into research findings.

Irwin/McGraw-Hill

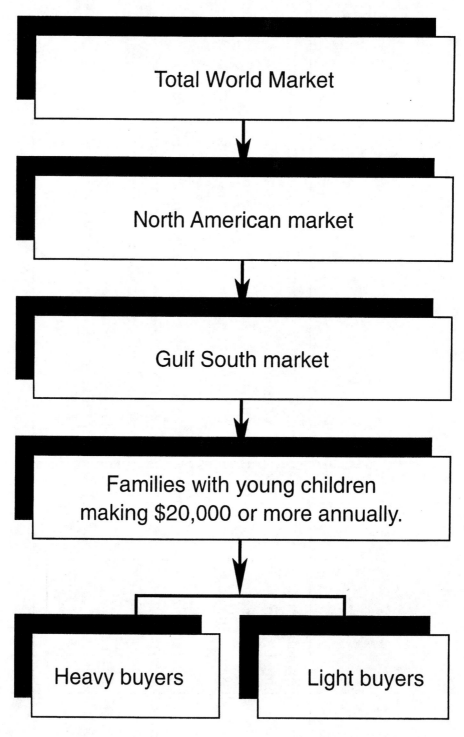

TM 6-2 Exhibit 6–2
Generalized Product Life Cycle

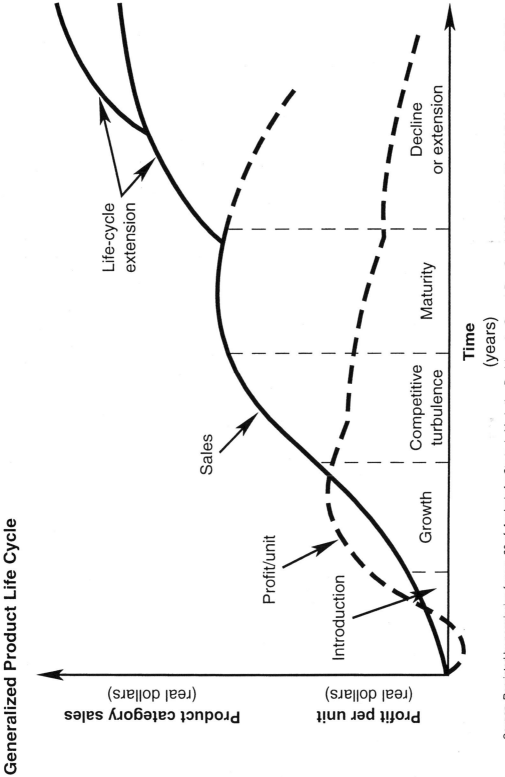

Life-cycle extension

Sales

Profit/unit

Introduction

Growth | Competitive turbulence | Maturity | Decline or extension

Time
(years)

Product category sales
(real dollars)

Profit per unit
(real dollars)

Source: Reprinted by permission from p. 60 of *Analysis for Strategic Marketing Decisions*, by George Day. Copyright © 1986 by West Publishing Company. All rights reserved.

Irwin/McGraw-Hill

The McGraw-Hill Companies, Inc., 1999

TM 6-3 Exhibit 6–3
More-Common Product Life-Cycle Curves

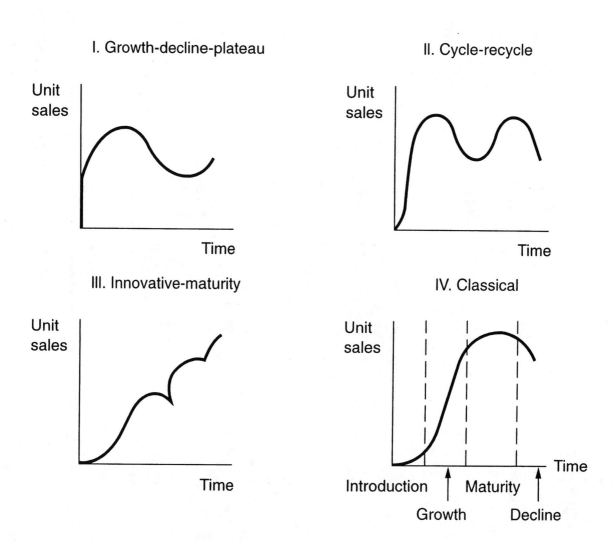

I. Growth-decline-plateau

II. Cycle-recycle

III. Innovative-maturity

IV. Classical

SOURCE: Adopted from J. E. Swan and D. R. Rink, "Effective Use of Industrial Product Life Cycle Trends," in *Marketing in the '80s* (New York: American Marketing Association, 1980), pp. 198–99.

TM 6-4 Exhibit 6-4
Expected Characteristics and Responses by Major Life-Cycle Stages

Stages in Product Life Cycle

Stage characteristics	Introduction	Growth	Shakeout	Mature	Decline
Market growth rate (constant dollars)	Moderate	High	Leveling off	Insignificant	Negative
Technical change in product design	High	Moderate	Limited	Limited	Limited
Segments	Few	Few to many	Few to many	Few to many	Few
Competitors	Small	Large	Decreasing	Limited	Few
Profitability	Negative	Large	Low	Large for high market-share holders	Low
Firm's normative responses					
Strategic marketing objectives	Stimulate primary demand	Build share	Build share	Hold share	Harvest
Product	Quality improvement	Continue quality improvement	Rationalize	Concentrate on features	No change
Product line	Narrow	Broad	Rationalize	Hold length of line	Reduce length of line
Price	Skimming versus penetration	Reduce	Reduce	Hold or reduce selectively	Reduce
Channels	Selective	Intensive	Intensive	Intensive	Selective
Communications	High	High	High	High to declining	Reduce

Irwin/McGraw-Hill

Relationship of Strategic Market Position Objective, Investment Levels, Profits, and Cash Flow to Individual Stages in the Product Life Cycle

Stage	Strategic market objective	Investments	Profits	Cash flow
Introduction	For both innovators and followers, accelerate overall market growth and product acceptance through awareness, trial, and product availability	Moderate to high for R&D, capacity, working capital, and marketing (sales and advertising)	Highly negative	Highly negative
Growth	Increase competitive position	High to very high	High	Negative
Shakeout	Improve/solidify competitive position	Moderate	Low to moderate	Low to moderate
Mature	Maintain position	Low	High	Moderate

Irwin/McGraw-Hill

TM 6-6 Exhibit 6–10
The Major Forces That Determine Industry Composition

Irwin/McGraw-Hill

TM 7-1 Exhibit 7-1
Sports Apparel Segmentation

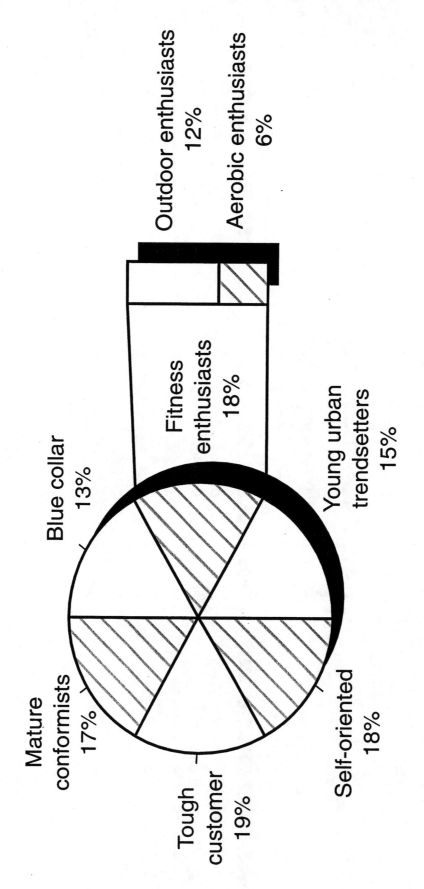

Outdoor enthusiasts
12%

Aerobic enthusiasts
6%

Fitness
enthusiasts
18%

Blue collar
13%

Young urban
trendsetters
15%

Mature
conformists
17%

Self-oriented
18%

Tough
customer
19%

Source: Vithala R. Rao and Joel H. Steckel, *The New Science of Marketing* (Chicago, Ill.: Irwin Professional Publishing, 1995), p. 302. Copyright 1995 by Irwin/McGraw-Hill. Reproduced with permission of the McGraw-Hill Companies.

Irwin/McGraw-Hill

The McGraw-Hill Companies, Inc., 1999

Descriptors Used to Segment Consumer and Industrial Markets

Descriptors	Consumer	Industrial
Physical		
Age	X	
Sex	X	
Household life cycle	X	
Income	X	
Occupation/position	X	
Education	X	
Geography	X	X
Event	X	
Race and ethnic origin	X	
Company size		X
Industry (SIC code)		X
General behavioral		
Lifestyle	X	
Social class	X	
Interests		
Purchase structure		X
Buying situation		X
Product-related behavior		
Product usage	X	X
Loyalty	X	X
Purchase predisposition	X	
Innovativeness	X	
Present customers	X	X
Customer needs	X	X

TM 7-3 Exhibit 7–7
**Steps in Constructing a Market-Attractiveness/Business-Position
Matrix for Evaluating Potential Target Markets**

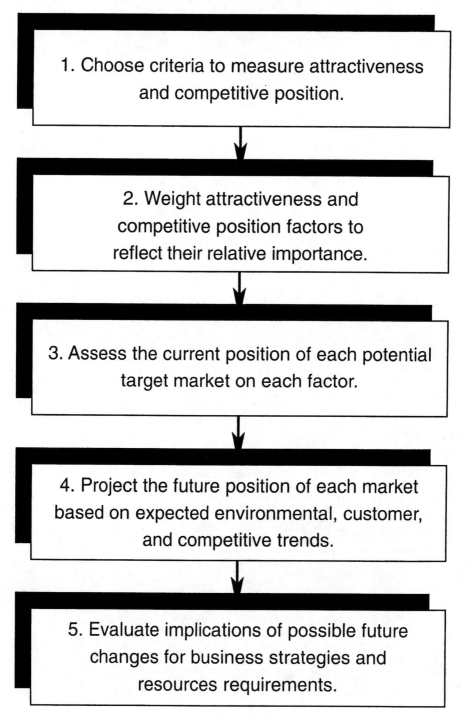

1. Choose criteria to measure attractiveness and competitive position.

2. Weight attractiveness and competitive position factors to reflect their relative importance.

3. Assess the current position of each potential target market on each factor.

4. Project the future position of each market based on expected environmental, customer, and competitive trends.

5. Evaluate implications of possible future changes for business strategies and resources requirements.

TM 7-4 Exhibit 7-8
Factors Underlying Market Attractiveness and Competitive Position

Market-attractiveness factors

Market/customer factors:
Size (dollars, units)
Market potential
Market growth rate
Stage in life cycle
Diversity of competitive offerings (potential for differentiation)
Customer loyalty/satisfaction with current offerings
Price elasticity
Bargaining power of customers
Cyclicality/seasonality of demand

Economic and technological factors:
Investment intensity
Industry capacity
Level and maturity of technology utilization
Ability to pass through effects of inflation
Barriers to entry/exit
Access to raw materials

Competitive factors:
Industry structure
Competitive groupings
Substitution threats
Perceived differentiation among competitors
Individual competitors' strengths

Environmental factors:
Regulatory climate
Degree of social acceptance

Competitive-position factors

Market position factors:
Relative market share
Rate of change in share
Perceived actual or potential differentiation (quality/service/price)
Breadth of current or planned product line
Company image

Economic and technological factors:
Relative cost position
Capacity utilization
Technological position
Patented technology (product or manufacturing)

Capabilities:
Management strength and depth
Financial
R&D/product development
Manufacturing
Marketing
Salesforce
Distribution system
Labor relations
Relations with regulators

Interactions with other segments:
Market synergies
Operating synergies

SOURCE: Adapted from George S. Day, *Analysis for Strategic Market Decisions* (St. Paul: West, 1986). pp. 198–99; and Derek F. Abell and John S. Hammond, *Strategic Market Planning Problems and Analytical Approaches* (Englewood Cliffs, N.J.: Prentice Hall, 1979), p. 214.

Irwin/McGraw-Hill   *The McGraw-Hill Companies, Inc., 1999*

Examples of Weights and Ratings Accorded Market Attractiveness and Business Strength Factors by Large Packaged Food Company

Attractiveness

Factor group	Weight	Rating*	Total
Market	50	8	400
Economic/technology	20	9	180
Competition	20	9	180
Environment	10	10	100
Total	100	36	860

Attractiveness rating = $\dfrac{860}{100}$ = 86

Business strengths

Factor group	Weight	Rating*	Total
Market position	20	9	180
Economic/technology	20	8	160
Capabilities	50	9	450
Interaction with other segments	10	10	100
Total	100	36	890

Business strength rating = $\dfrac{890}{100}$ = 89

*Rating scale = 0–10.

Irwin/McGraw-Hill

© *The McGraw-Hill Companies, Inc., 1999*

Matrix Showing the Competitive Position of a Packaged Food Company in a Given Segment Based on a Matching of Business Strengths and Market Attractiveness

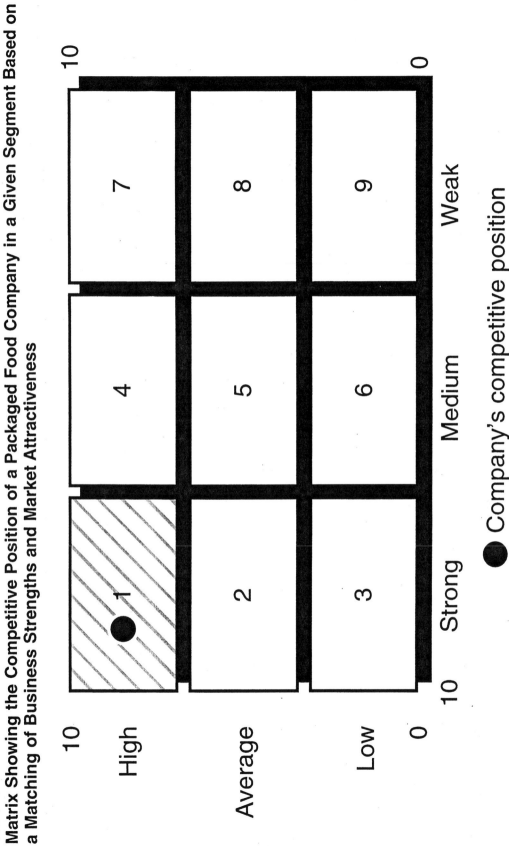

● Company's competitive position

Implications of Alternative Positions within the Market-Attractiveness/Business-Position Matrix for Target Market Selection, Strategic Objectives, and Resource Allocation

Competitive position

Market Attractiveness	Strong	Medium	Weak
High	DESIRABLE POTENTIAL TARGET Protect position: • Invest to grow at maximum digestible rate • Concentrate on maintaining strength	DESIRABLE POTENTIAL TARGET Invest to build: • Challenge for leadership • Build selectively on strengths • Reinforce vulnerable areas	Build selectively: • Specialize around limited strengths • Seek ways to overcome weaknesses • Withdraw if indications of sustainable growth are lacking
Medium	DESIRABLE POTENTIAL TARGET Build selectively: • Emphasize profitability by increasing productivity • Build up ability to counter competition	Manage for earnings: • Protect existing strengths • Invest to improve position only in areas where risk is low	Limited expansion or harvest: • Look for ways to expand without high risk; otherwise, minimize investment and focus operations
Low	Protect and refocus: • Defend strengths • Seek ways to increase current earnings without speeding market's decline	Manage for earnings: • Protect position • Minimize investment	Divest: • Sell when possible to maximize cash value • Meantime, cut fixed costs and avoid further investment

SOURCE: Adapted from George S. Day, *Analysis for Strategic Market Decisions* (St. Paul: West, 1986), p. 204; D. F. Abell and J. S. Hammond, *Strategic Market Planning Problems and Analytical Approaches* (Englewood Cliffs, N.J.: Prentice Hall, 1979); and S. J. Robinson, R. E. Hitchens, and D. P. Wade, "The Directional Policy Matrix: Tool for Strategic Planning," *Long Range Planning* 11 (1978), pp. 8–15.

Irwin/McGraw-Hill

1996 Ford Expedition vs. GM Suburban on Selected Number of Physical Dimensions

Feature	Expedition	Suburban
Seating capacity	9	9
Cargo capacity	115 cu. ft.	149.5 cu. ft.
Engine	4.6 liter, V-8	5.7 liter, V-8
City mileage	14 mpg	13 mpg
Highway mileage	18 mpg	17 mpg
Length	204.6 inches	220 inches
Price	$24,000–36,000	$24,682–38,000

SOURCE: Aaron Lucchetti, "Ford's New Expedition Heads into Suburban's Terrain," *The Wall Street Journal*, June 24, 1996, p. B1. Reprinted by permission of the Wall Street Journal, © 1996 Dow Jones & Company, Inc. All rights reserved worldwide.

Irwin/McGraw-Hill

The McGraw-Hill Companies, Inc., 1999

Physical positioning

- Technical orientation
- Physical characteristics
- Objective measures
- Data readily available
- Physical brand properties
- Large number of dimensions
- Represents impact of product specs and price
- Direct R&D implications

Perceptual analyses

- Consumer orientation
- Perceptual attributes
- Perceptual measures
- Need marketing research
- Perceptual brand positions and positioning intensities
- Limited number of dimensions
- Represents impact of products specs and communication
- R&D implications need to be interpreted

© *The McGraw-Hill Companies, Inc., 1999*

Irwin/McGraw-Hill

TM 8-3 Exhibit 8–4
Steps in the Positioning Process

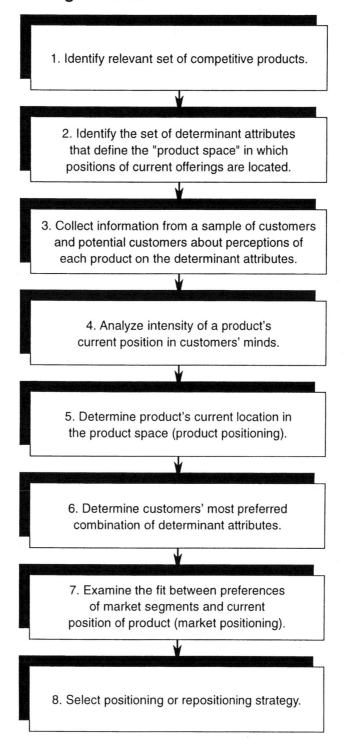

1. Identify relevant set of competitive products.

2. Identify the set of determinant attributes that define the "product space" in which positions of current offerings are located.

3. Collect information from a sample of customers and potential customers about perceptions of each product on the determinant attributes.

4. Analyze intensity of a product's current position in customers' minds.

5. Determine product's current location in the product space (product positioning).

6. Determine customers' most preferred combination of determinant attributes.

7. Examine the fit between preferences of market segments and current position of product (market positioning).

8. Select positioning or repositioning strategy.

Irwin/McGraw-Hill

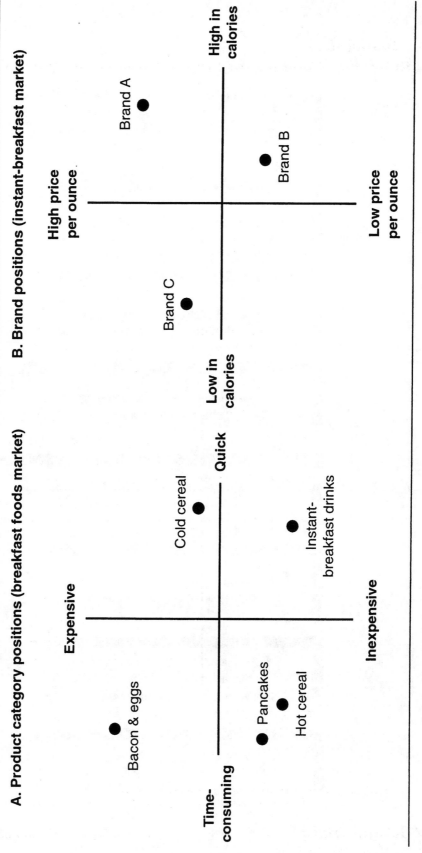

A. Product category positions (breakfast foods market)

Expensive

Time-consuming

Quick

Low in calories

B. Brand positions (instant-breakfast market)

High price per ounce

High in calories

Low price per ounce

Brand A

Brand B

Brand C

Cold cereal

Instant-breakfast drinks

Bacon & eggs

Pancakes

Hot cereal

Inexpensive

Source: Adapted from P. S. Busch and M. J. Houston, *Marketing Strategic Foundations* (Burr Ridge, Ill.: Richard D. Irwin, 1985), p. 430.

Irwin/McGraw-Hill

The McGraw-Hill Companies, Inc., 1999

TM 8-5 Exhibit 8–6
Perceptual Map of Women's Clothing Retailers in Washington, D.C.

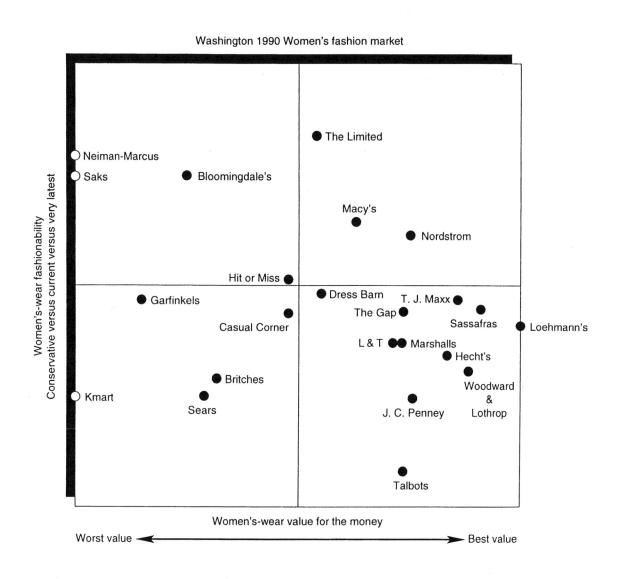

Washington 1990 Women's fashion market

SOURCE: Adapted from Douglas Tigert and Stephen Arnold, "Nordstrom: How Good Are They?" *Babson College Retailing Research Reports*, September 1990, as shown in Michael Levy and Barton A. Weitz, *Retailing Management* (Burr Ridge, Ill.: Richard D. Irwin, 1992), p. 205.

Irwin/McGraw-Hill   *The McGraw-Hill Companies, Inc., 1999*

**Perceptual Map of Women's Clothing Retailers in Washington, D.C.,
Showing the Ideal Points of a Segment of Consumers**

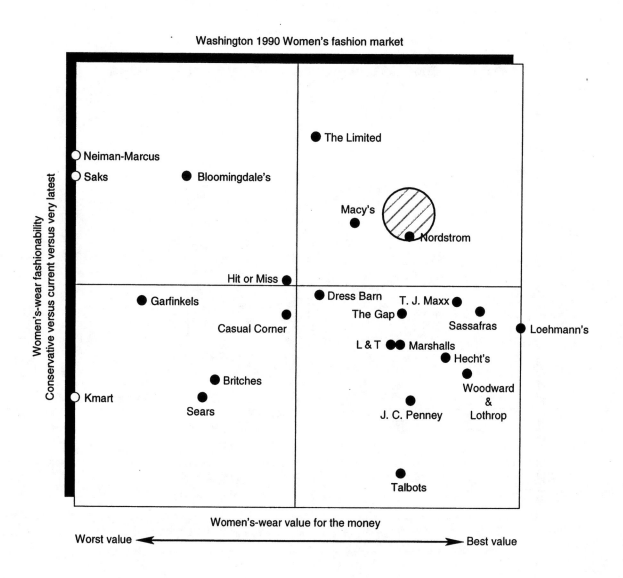

Washington 1990 Women's fashion market

SOURCE: Adapted from Douglas Tigert and Stephen Arnold, "Nordstrom: How Good Are They?"
Babson College Retailing Research Reports, September 1990.

Irwin/McGraw-Hill   *The McGraw-Hill Companies, Inc., 1999*

Perceptual Map of Women's Clothing Retailers in Washington, D.C., Showing Five Segments Based on Ideal Points

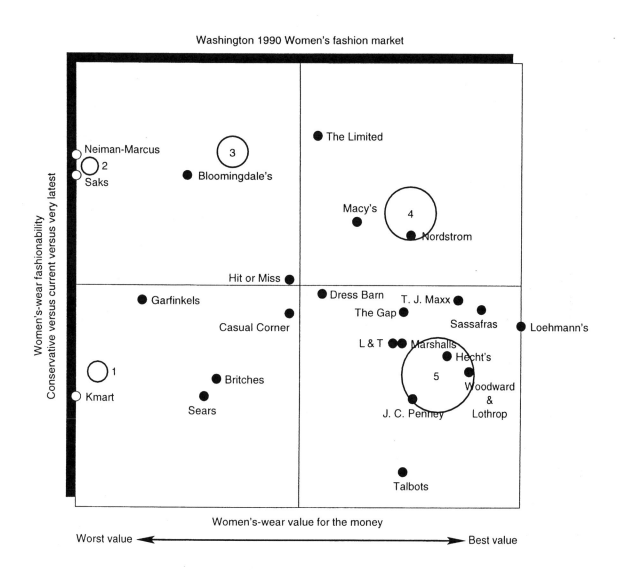

Washington 1990 Women's fashion market

Women's-wear fashionability
Conservative versus current versus very latest

Women's-wear value for the money

Worst value ← → Best value

SOURCE: Adapted from Douglas Tigert and Stephen Arnold, "Nordstrom: How Good Are They?"
Babson College Retailing Research Reports, September 1990.

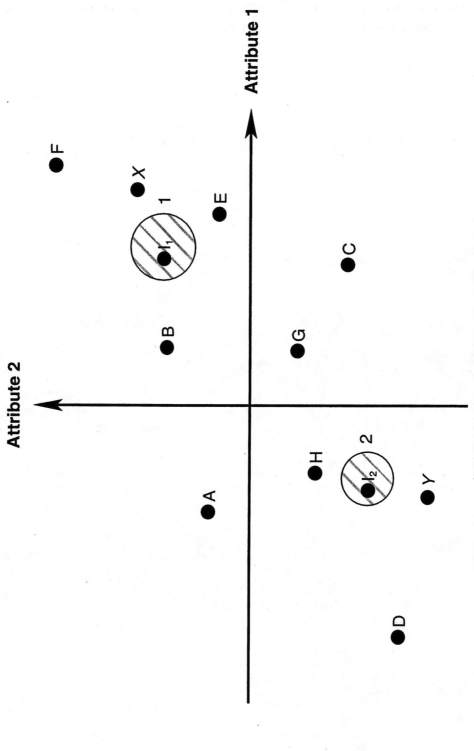

NOTE: Circles identify ideal points 1 and 2.

Irwin/McGraw-Hill

Illustration of Purchase of Intent Shares before and after Introduction of New Product (in Percent)

| | | | | Existing brands | | | | | | New brand |
		A	B	C	D	E	F	G	H	X or Y
Current	Segment 1	3.9	24.0	6.4	1.3	38.1	12.2	9.6	4.4	
	Segment 2	11.1	4.5	5.9	14.0	2.9	1.4	10.3	49.9	
	Total	6.3	17.5	6.2	5.5	26.4	8.6	9.8	19.6	
With X	Segment 1	2.9	18.0	4.8	1.0	28.6	9.2	7.2	3.3	25.0
	Segment 2	10.9	4.4	5.8	13.7	2.9	1.4	10.1	48.9	1.9
	Total	5.6	13.5	5.1	5.2	20.0	6.6	8.2	18.5	17.3
With Y	Segment 1	3.8	23.4	6.3	1.3	37.2	11.9	9.4	4.3	2.4
	Segment 2	8.0	3.3	4.2	10.1	2.1	1.0	7.4	36.0	27.8
	Total	5.2	16.7	5.6	4.2	25.5	8.3	8.7	14.9	10.9

Categories of New Products Defined According to Their Degree of Newness to the Company and Customers in the Target Market

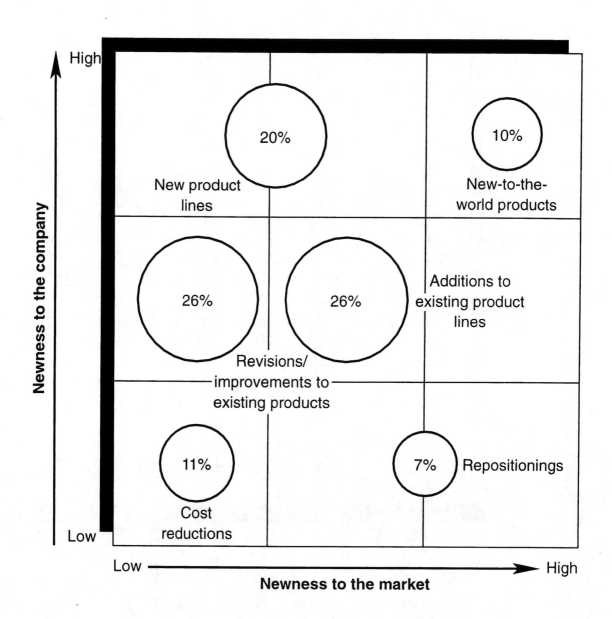

SOURCE: New Products Management for the 1980s (New York: Booz, Allen & Hamilton, 1982), p. 8.

TM 9-2 Exhibit 9–2
Strategic Objectives Attained by Successful New Market Entries

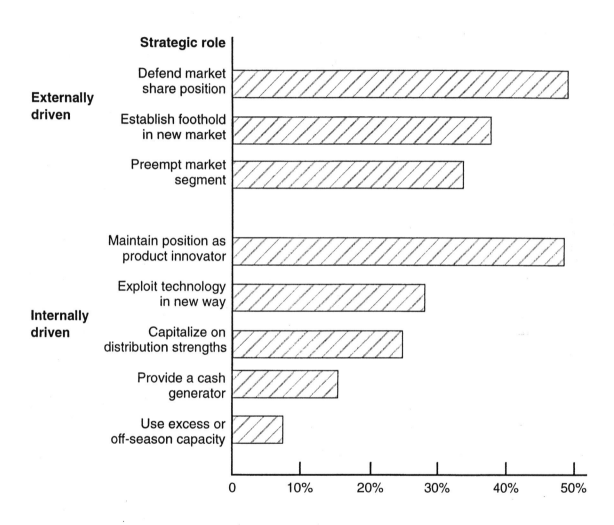

SOURCE: *New Products Management for the 1980s* (New York: Booz, Allen & Hamilton, 1982), p. 11.

Irwin/McGraw-Hill   *The McGraw-Hill Companies, Inc., 1999*

TM 9-3 Exhibit 9-3
Types of New Market Entries Appropriate for Different Strategic Objectives

Objective	New entry
Maintain position as a product innovator	New-to-the-world products; improvements or revisions to existing products
Defend a current market-share position	Improvements or revisions to existing products; additions to existing product line; cost reductions
Establish a foothold in a future new market; preempt a market segment	New-to-the-world products; additions to existing product line; repositionings
Exploit technology in a new way	New-to-the-world products; new product line; additions to or revision of existing product line
Capitalize on distribution strengths	New-to-the-world products; new product line; additions to or revisions of existing product line
Provide a cash generator	Additions to or revisions of existing product line; repositionings; cost reductions
Use excess or off-season capacity	New-to-the-world product; new product line

Irwin/McGraw-Hill

Potential Advantages of Pioneer and Follower Strategies

Pioneer

- Economies of scale and experience.
- High switching costs for early adopters.
- Ability to define the rules of the game.
- Distribution advantage.
- Influence on consumer choice criteria and attitudes.
- Possibility of preempting scarce resources.

Follower

- Ability to take advantage of pioneer's positioning mistakes.
- Ability to take advantage of pioneer's product mistakes.
- Ability to take advantage of pioneer's marketing mistakes.
- Ability to take advantage of pioneer's limited resources.
- Ability to take advantage of the latest technology.

Irwin/McGraw-Hill

Marketing Strategy Elements Pursued by Successful Pioneers, Fast Followers, and Late Entrants

These marketers . . .	are characterized by one or more of these strategy elements:
Successful pioneers	• Large entry scale • Broad product line • High product quality • Heavy promotional expenditures

Successful fast followers	• Larger entry scale than the pioneer
	• Leapfrogging the pioneer with superior:
	    Product technology
	    Product quality
	      Customer service

Successful late entrants	• Focus on peripheral target markets or niches

Irwin/McGraw-Hill

TM 9-6 Exhibit 9-6
Situations Favoring Alternative Marketing Strategies for New Product Pioneers

Alternative marketing strategies

	Mass-market penetration	Niche penetration	Skimming and early withdrawal
Market characteristics	• Large potential demand • Homogeneous customers • Short diffusion process	• Large potential demand • Fragmented market • Short adoption process	• Limited potential demand • Long adoption process • Demand is price inelastic
Product characteristics	• Product technology patentable or difficult to copy • Limited sources of supply • Complex production process	• Product technology offers little patent protection • Many sources of supply • Relatively simple production process	• Product technology offers little patent protection • Many sources of supply • Relatively simple production process
Competitor characteristics	• Few potential competitors • Potential competitors have limited resources and competencies	• Many potential competitors • Some potential competitors have substantial resources and competencies	• Many potential competitors • Some potential competitors have substantial resources and competencies
Firm characteristics	• Strong product engineering skills • Strong marketing skills and resources • Sufficient financial and organizational resources to build capacity in advance of growth in demand	• Limited product engineering skills and resources • Limited marketing skills and resources • Insufficient financial or organizational resources to build capacity in advance of growing demand	• Strong basic R&D and new product development skills • Good sales and promotional skills • Limited financial or organizational resources to commit to building capacity in advance of growth in demand

Irwin/McGraw-Hill

Objectives of Strategic Marketing Programs for Pioneers

Alternative strategic marketing programs

Strategic objectives	Mass-market penetration	Niche penetration	Skimming; early withdrawal
Short-term objectives	• Maximize number of triers and adopters in total market; invest heavily to build future volume and share	• Maximize number of triers and adopters in target segment; limited investment to build volume and share in chosen niche	• Obtain as many adopters as possible with limited investment; maintain high margins to recoup product development and commercialization costs as soon as possible
Intermediate-term objectives	• Attempt to preempt competition; maintain leading share position even if some sacrifice of margins is necessary in short term as new competitors enter	• Maintain leading share position in target segment even if some sacrifice of short-term margins is necessary	• Maximize ROI; withdraw from market when increasing competition puts downward pressure on margins
Long-term objectives	• Maximize ROI	• Maximize ROI	• Withdraw

TM 9-8 Exhibit 9–9
Components of Strategic Marketing Programs for Pioneers

Strategic objectives and tasks	Alternative strategic marketing programs		
	Mass-market penetration	Niche penetration	Skimming; early withdrawal
Increase customers' awareness and willingness to buy	• Heavy advertising to generate awareness among customers in mass market	• Heavy advertising directed at target segment to generate awareness	• Limited advertising to generate awareness, particularly among least price-sensitive early adopters
	• Extensive salesforce efforts to win new adopters	• Extensive salesforce efforts focused on potential customers in target segment	• Extensive salesforce efforts, particularly focused on largest potential adopters
	• Extensive introductory sales promotions to induce trial (sampling, couponing, quantity discounts)	• Extensive introductory sales promotions to induce trial, but focused on target segment	• Limited use, if any, of introductory sales promotions
	• Quickly expand offerings to appeal to multiple segments	• Additional product development limited to improvements to increase appeal to target segment	• Little, if any, additional development within the product category
	• Offer free trial, liberal return, or extended warranty policies to reduce customers' perceived risk	• Offer free trial, liberal return, or extended warranty policies to reduce target customers' perceived risk	• Offer free trial, liberal return, or extended warranty policies to reduce target customers' perceived risk
Increase customers's ability to buy	• Penetration pricing; or bring out lower-priced versions in anticipation of competitive entries	• Penetration pricing, or bring out lower-priced versions in anticipation of competitive entries	• Skimming pricing
	• Extended credit terms to encourage initial purchases	• Extended credit terms to encourage initial purchases	• Extended credit terms to encourage initial purchases
	• Heavy use of trade promotions aimed at gaining extensive distribution	• Trade promotions aimed at gaining distribution pertinent for reaching target segment	• Limited use of trade promotions
	• Offer engineering, installation, and training services to increase new product's compatibility with customers' current operations	• Offer engineering installation, and training services to increase new product's compatibility with customers' current operations	• Offer limited engineering, installation, and services as necessary to overcome customers' objections

TM 10-1 Exhibit 10-1
Market Shares of the Leader and Followers over the Life Cycle of a Hypothetical Market

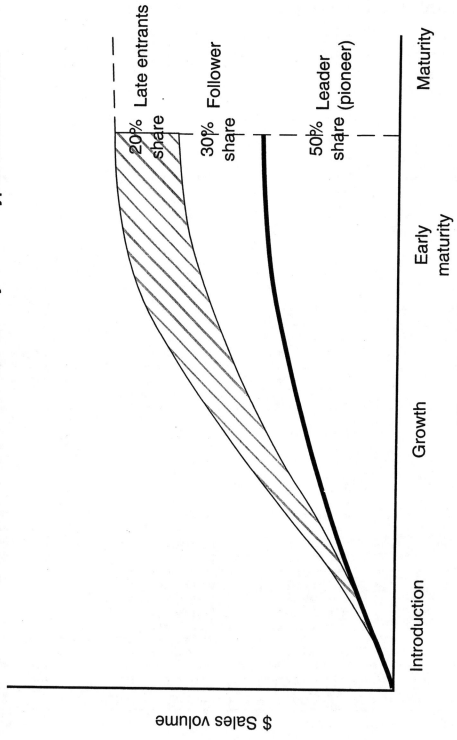

Life-cycle stages

SOURCE: Reprinted by permission from p. 60 of *Analysis for Strategic Market Decisions* by George S. Day; copyright © 1986 by West Publishing Company.

Irwin/McGraw-Hill

The McGraw-Hill Companies, Inc., 1999

TM 10-2 Exhibit 10–3
The Proportion of Market Leaders in the PIMS Database Who Lost Market Share, by Size of Their Initial Share

Leader's initial market share	Percent losing share
Under 20%	16%
20–29	24
30–39	34
40–49	41
Over 50	45
All leaders	31

SOURCE: Adapted with permission of The Free Press, an imprint of Simon & Schuster Inc. from *The PIMS Principles: Linking Strategy to Performance* by Robert D. Buzzell and Bradley T. Gale. Copyright © 1987 by The Free Press.

SOURCE: Adapted with permission of The Free Press, an imprint of Simon & Schuster Inc. from *The PIMS Principles: Linking Strategy to Performance* by Robert D. Buzzell and Bradley T. Gale. Copyright © 1987 by The Free Press.

Irwin/McGraw-Hill   *The McGraw-Hill Companies, Inc., 1999*

Marketing objectives	Possible marketing actions
Retain current customers by:	
• Maintaining/improving satisfaction and loyalty	• Increase attention to quality control as output expands. • Continue product modification and improvement efforts to increase customer benefits and/or reduce costs. • Focus advertising on stimulation of selective demand; stress product's superior features and benefits; reminder advertising. • Increase salesforce's servicing of current accounts; consider formation of national or key account representatives for major customers; consider replacing independent manufacturers' reps with company salespeople. • Expand postsale service capabilities; develop or expand company's own service force, or develop training programs for distributors' and dealers' service people; expand parts inventory; consider development of customer service hotline.
• Encourage/simplify repeat purchase	• Expand production capacity in advance of increasing demand to avoid stockouts. • Improve inventory control and logistics systems to reduce delivery times. • Continue to build distribution channels; use periodic trade promotions to gain more extensive retail coverage and maintain shelf facings; strengthen relationships with strongest distributors/dealers. • Consider negotiating long-term requirements contracts with major customers. • Consider developing automatic reorder systems for major customers. • Consider logistical alliances with major customers.
• Reduce attractiveness of switching	• Develop a second brand or product line with features or price more appealing to a specific segment of current customers (*flanker strategy*). • Develop multiple line extensions or brand offerings targeted to the needs of several user segments in the market (*market expansion, mobile strategy*). • Meet or beat lower prices or heavier promotional efforts by competitors—or try to preempt such efforts by potential competitors—when necessary to retain customers and when lower unit costs allow (*confrontation strategy*).
Stimulate selective demand among later adopters by:	
• Head-to-head positioning against competitive offerings or potential offerings	• Develop a second brand or product line with features or price more appealing to a specific segment of potential customers (*flanker strategy*). • Make product modifications or improvements to match or beat superior competitive offerings (*confrontation strategy*). • Meet or beat lower prices or heavier promotional efforts by competitors when necessary to retain customers and when lower unit costs allow (*confrontation strategy*). • When resources are limited relative to competitor's, consider withdrawing from smaller or slower-growing segments to focus product development and promotional efforts on higher-potential segments threatened by competitor (*contraction or strategic withdrawal strategy*).
• Differentiated positioning against competitive offerings or potential offerings	• Develop multiple line extensions or brand offerings targeted to the needs of various potential user applications or geographical segments within the market (*market expansion or mobile strategy*). • Build unique distribution channels to more effectively reach specific segments of potential customers (*market expansion or mobile strategy*). • Design multiple advertising and/or sales promotion campaigns targeted at specific segments of potential customers (*market expansion or mobile strategy*).

TM 10-4 Exhibit 10–5
Strategic Choices for Share Leaders in Growth Markets

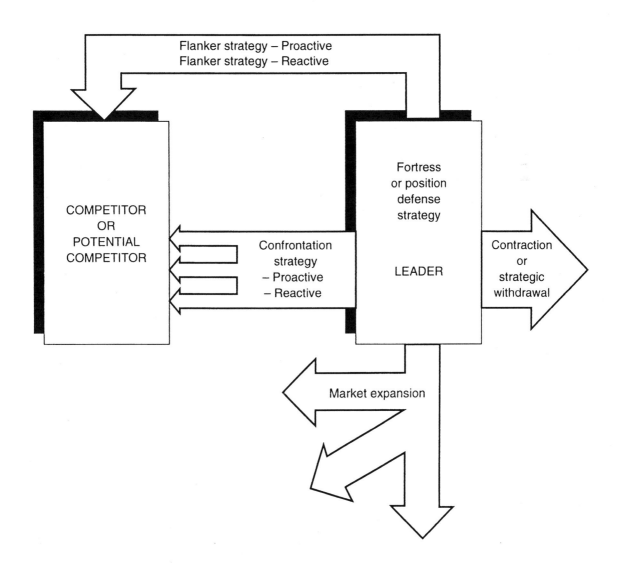

SOURCE: Adapted from P. Kotler and R. Singh, "Marketing Warfare in the 1980s," *Journal of Business Strategy,* Winter 1981, pp. 30–41.

Irwin/McGraw-Hill   *The McGraw-Hill Companies, Inc., 1999*

TM 10-5 Exhibit 10–6
Marketing Objectives of Share-Maintenance Strategies in Growth Markets

Share maintenance strategies

Fortress or position defense	Flanker	Confrontation	Market expansion	Contraction or strategic withdrawal
Increase satisfaction, loyalty, and repeat purchase among current customers by building on existing strengths; appeal to late adopters with same attributes and benefits offered to early adopters.	Protect against loss of specific segment of current customers by developing a second entry that covers a weakness in original offering; improve ability to attract new customers with specific needs or purchase criteria different from those of early adopters.	Protect against loss of share among current customers by meeting or beating a head-to-head competitive offering; improve ability to win new customers who might otherwise be attracted to competitor's offering.	Increase ability to attract new customers by developing new product offerings or line extensions aimed at a variety of new applications and user segments; improve ability to retain current customers as market fragments.	Increase ability to attract new customers in selected high-growth segments by focusing offerings and resources on those segments; withdraw from smaller or slower-growing segments to conserve resources.

Irwin/McGraw-Hill

Marketing Actions to Achieve Share-Growth Objectives

Marketing objectives	Possible marketing actions

Capture repeat/replacement purchases from current customers of the leader or other target competitor by:
 	
• Head-to-head positioning against competitor's offering in primary target market
	• Develop products with features and/or performance levels superior to those of the target competitor.
	• Draw on superior product design, process engineering, and supplier relationships to achieve lower unit costs.
	• Set prices below target competitor's for comparable level of quality or performance, but only if flow-cost position is achieved.
	• Outspend the target competitor on promotion aimed at stimulating selective demand:
	    Comparative advertising appeals directed at gaining a more favorable positioning than the target competitor's brand enjoys among customers in the mass market.
	    Sales promotions to encourage trial if offering's quality or performance is perceptively better than target competitor's, or induce brand switching.
	    Build more extensive and/or better-trained salesforce than target competitor's.
	• Outspend the target competitor on trade promotion to attain more extensive retail coverage, better shelf space, and/or representation by the best distributors/dealers.
	• Outperform the target competitor on customer service:
	    Develop superior production scheduling, inventory control, and logistics systems to minimize delivery times and stockouts.
	    Develop superior postsales service capabilities; build a more extensive company service force, or provide better training programs for distributor/dealer service people than target competitor.
	• If resources are limited, engage in one or more of the preceding actions (such as an advertising blitz or sales or trade promotions) on a sporadic basis in selected territories (*guerrilla attack strategy*).

• Technological differentiation from target competitor's offering in its primary target market	• Develop a new generation of products based on different technology that offers superior performance or additional benefits desired by current and potential customers in the mass market (*leapfrog strategy*).

Marketing objectives	Possible marketing actions
	• Build awareness, preference, and replacement demand through heavy introductory promotion:
	Comparative advertising stressing product's superiority.
	Sales promotions to stimulate trial or encourage switching.
	Extensive, well-trained salesforce; heavy use of product demonstrations in sales presentations.
	• Build adequate distribution through trade promotions and dealer training programs.
Stimulate selective demand among later adopters by:	
• Head-to-head positioning against target competitor's offering in established market segments	• See preceding actions.
• Differentiated positioning focused on untapped or underdeveloped segments	• Develop a differentiated brand or product line with unique features or price that is more appealing to a major segment of potential customers whose needs are not met by existing offerings (*flanking strategy*).
	or
	• Develop multiple line extensions or brand offerings with features or prices targeted to the unique needs and preferences of several smaller potential applications or regional segments (*encirclement strategy*).
	• Design advertising, personal selling, and/or sales promotion campaigns that address specific interests and concerns of potential customers in one or multiple underdeveloped segments to stimulate selective demand.
	• Build unique distribution channels to more effectively reach potential customers in one or multiple underdeveloped segments.
	• Design service programs to reduce the perceived risks of trial and/or solve the unique problems faced by potential customers in one or multiple underdeveloped segments (for example, systems engineering, installation, operator training, or extended warranties).

TM 10-7 Exhibit 10–8
Strategic Choices for Challengers in Growth Markets

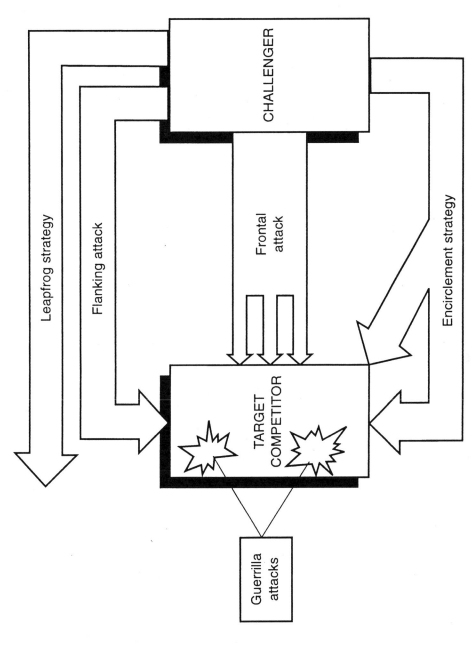

SOURCE: Adapted from P. Kotler and R. Singh, "Marketing Warfare in the 1980s." Reprinted with permission from *Journal of Business Strategy*, Winter 1981, pp. 30–41. Copyright © Warren, Gorham & Lambert, Inc., 210 South Street, Boston, MA 02111. All rights reserved.

Irwin/McGraw-Hill

The McGraw-Hill Companies, Inc., 1999

TM 10-8 Exhibit 10–9
Marketing Objectives of Share-Growth Strategies

Share-growth strategies

Frontal attack	Leapfrog	Flank attack	Encirclement	Guerrilla attack
Capture substantial repeat/replacement purchases from target competitor's current customers; attract new customers among later adopters by offering lower price or more attractive features.	Induce current customers in mass market to replace their current brand with superior new offering; attract new customers by providing enhanced benefits.	Attract substantial share of new customers in one or more major segments where customer's needs are different from those of early adopters in the mass market.	Attract a substantial share of new customers in a variety of smaller, specialized segments where customers' needs or preferences differ from those of early adopters in the mass market.	Capture a modest share of repeat/replacement purchases in several market segments or territories; attract a share of new customers in a number of existing segments.

Irwin/McGraw-Hill

© *The McGraw-Hill Companies, Inc., 1999*

TM 10-9 Exhibit 10–12
Strategic Changes Made by Challengers That Gained or Lost Market Share

Strategic changes	Share-gaining challengers	Share-losing challengers
Relative product quality scores	+1.8	−0.6
New products as a percentage of sales	+0.1	−0.5
Relative price	+0.3	+0.2
Marketing expenditures (adjusted for market growth)		
Salesforce	+9.0%	−8.0%
Advertising		
Consumer products	+13.0%	−9.0%
Industrial products	−1.0	−14.0
Promotion		
Consumer products	+13.0%	−5.0%
Industrial products	+7.0	−10.0

SOURCE: Adapted with permission of The Free Press, an imprint of Simon & Schuster Inc. from *The PIMS Principles: Linking Strategy to Performance* by Robert D. Buzzell and Bradley T. Gale. Copyright ©1987 by The Free Press.

Irwin/McGraw-Hill

The McGraw-Hill Companies, Inc., 1999

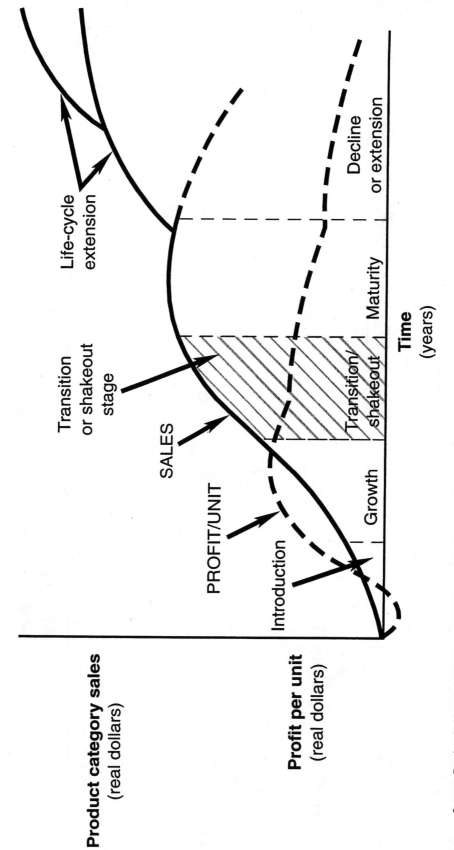

SOURCE: Reprinted with permission from p. 60 of *Analysis for Strategic Market Decisions*, by George S. Day, copyright © 1986 by West Publishing Company. All rights reserved.

Irwin/McGraw-Hill

The McGraw-Hill Companies, Inc., 1999

TM 11-2 Exhibit 11–3
Three Strategic Disciplines of Market Leaders and the Traits of Businesses That Implement Them Effectively

Disciplines

Company traits	Operational excellence	Product leadership	Customer intimacy
Core business processes	Sharpen distribution systems and provide no-hassle service	Nurture ideas, translate them into products, and market them skillfully	Provide solutions and help customers run their businesses
Structure	Has strong, central authority and a finite level of empowerment	Acts in an ad hoc, organic, loosely knit, and ever-changing way	Pushes empowerment close to customer contact
Management systems	Maintain standard operating procedures	Reward individuals' innovative capacity and new product success	Measure the cost of providing service and of maintaining customer loyalty
Culture	Acts predictably and believes "one size fits all"	Experiments and thinks "out-of-the-box"	Is flexible and thinks "have it your way"

SOURCE: Michael Treacy, Fred Wiersema, "How Market Leaders Keep Their Edge," *Fortune*, February 6, 1995, p. 96. Excerpted from *The Discipline of Market Leaders*, © 1996 by Michael Treacy, Fred Wiersema and CSC Index, Inc. Reprinted by permission of Addison Wesley Longman.

Irwin/McGraw-Hill

The McGraw-Hill Companies, Inc., 1999

TM 11-3 Exhibit 11—4
Dimensions of Product Quality

- Performance   How well does the washing machine wash clothes?
- Durability   How long will the lawn mower last?
- Conformance with specifications   What is the incidence of product defects?
- Features   Does an airline flight offer a movie and dinner?
- Reliability   Will each visit to a restaurant result in consistent quality?
                                       What percentage of the time will a product perform satisfactorily?
- Serviceability   Is the product easy to service?
                                       Is the service system efficient, competent, and convenient?
- Fit and finish   Does the product look and feel like a quality product?
- Brand name   Is this a name that customers associate with quality?
                                       What is the brand's image?

SOURCE: Adapted from "What Does 'Product Quality' Really Mean?" by David A. Garvin, *Sloan Management Review*, Fall 1984, pp. 25–43. Copyright © 1984 by the Sloan Management Review Association. All rights reserved. Used by permission of the publisher.

Irwin/McGraw-Hill

The McGraw-Hill Companies, Inc., 1999

Dimensions of Service Quality

- Tangibles   Appearance of physical facilities, equipment, personnel, and communications materials

- Reliability   Ability to perform the promised service dependably and accurately

- Responsiveness   Willingness to help customers and provide prompt service

- Assurance   Knowledge and courtesy of employees and their ability to convey trust and confidence

- Empathy   Caring, individualized attention the firm provides its customers

SOURCE: Valarie A. Zeithaml, A. Parasuraman, and Leonard L. Berry, *Delivering Quality Service: Balancing Customer Perceptions and Expectations* (New York: Free Press, 1990), p. 26. Reprinted with permission.

Perceived Importance of Service Quality Dimensions in Four Different Industries

	Mean importance rating on 10-point scale*	Percentage of respondents indicating dimension is most important
Credit card customers (n = 187)		
Tangibles	7.43	0.6
Reliability	9.45	48.6
Responsiveness	9.37	19.8
Assurance	9.25	17.5
Empathy	9.09	13.6
Repair and maintenance customers (n = 183)		
Tangibles	8.48	1.2
Reliability	9.64	57.2
Responsiveness	9.54	19.9
Assurance	9.62	12.0
Empathy	9.30	9.6
Long-distance telephone customers (n = 184)		
Tangibles	7.14	0.6
Reliability	9.67	60.6
Responsiveness	9.57	16.0
Assurance	9.29	12.6
Empathy	9.25	10.3
Bank customers (n = 177)		
Tangibles	8.56	1.1
Reliability	9.44	42.1
Responsiveness	9.34	18.0
Assurance	9.18	13.6
Empathy	9.30	25.1

*Scale ranges from 1 (not at all important) to 10 (extremely important).

SOURCE: Reprinted with permission of The Free Press, a division of Macmillan, Inc. from *Delivering Quality Service: Balancing Customer Perceptions and Expectations* by Valarie A. Zeithaml, A. Parasuraman, and Leonard L. Berry. Copyright © 1990 by The Free Press.

TM 11-6 Exhibit 11–7
Determinants of Perceived Service Quality

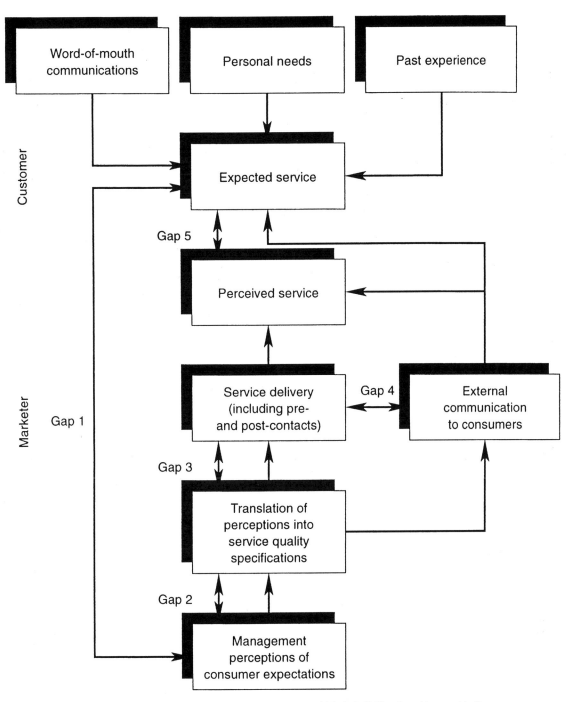

Source: Reprinted with permission from A. Parasuraman, Valarie A. Zeithaml, and Leonard L. Berry,
"A Conceptual Model of Service Quality and Its Implications for Future Research,"
Journal of Marketing, Fall 1985, p. 44. Published by the American Marketing Association.

Irwin/McGraw-Hill   *The McGraw-Hill Companies, Inc., 1999*

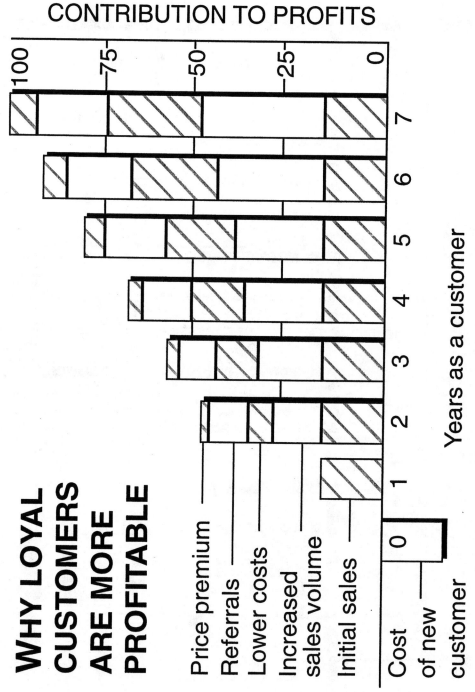

WHY LOYAL CUSTOMERS ARE MORE PROFITABLE

CONTRIBUTION TO PROFITS

Price premium
Referrals
Lower costs
Increased sales volume
Initial sales

Cost of new customer

Years as a customer

SOURCE: Rahul Jacob, "Why Some Customers Are More Equal Than Others," *Fortune*, September 19, 1994, p. 220.

Irwin/McGraw-Hill

The McGraw-Hill Companies, Inc., 1999

Factors Affecting the Attractiveness of Declining Markets

	Environmental attractiveness	
	Hospitable	**Inhospitable**
Conditions of demand		
Speed of decline	Very slow	Rapid or erratic
Certainty of decline	100% certain predictable patterns	Great uncertainty, erratic patterns
Pockets of enduring demand	Several or major ones	No niches
Product differentiation	Brand loyalty	Commonditylike products
Price stability	Stable, price premiums attainable	Very unstable, pricing below costs
Exit barriers		
Reinvestment requirements	None	High, often mandatory and involving capital assets
Excess capacity	Little	Substantial
Asset age	Mostly old assets	Sizable new assets and old ones not retired
Resale markets for assets	Easy to convert or sell	No markets available, substantial costs to retire
Shared facilities	Few; freestanding plants	Substantial and interconnected with important businesses
Vertical integration	Little	Substantial
Single-product competitors	None	Several large companies
Rivalry determinants		
Customer industries	Fragmented, weak	Strong bargaining power
Customer switching costs	High	Minimal
Diseconomies of scale	None	Substantial penalty
Dissimilar strategic groups	Few	Several in same target markets

SOURCE: Kathryn Rudie Harrigan and Michael E. Porter, "End-Game Strategies for Declining Industries," *Harvard Business Review,* July–August 1983, p. 117. Reprinted by permission of *Harvard Business Review.* Copyright 1983 by the President and Fellows of Harvard College, all rights reserved.

TM 12-1 Exhibit 12–2
Administrative Factors Related to the Successful Implementation of Business Strategies

Types of Business Strategy

Administrative factor	Prospector	Differentiated defender	Low-cost defender
SBU autonomy	Relatively high level	Moderate level	Relatively low level
Shared programs and synergy	Relatively little synergy—few shared programs	Little synergy in areas central to differentiation—shared programs elsewhere	High level of synergy and shared programs
Evaluation and reward systems	High incentives based on sales and share growth	High incentives based on profits or ROI	High incentives based on profits or ROI

Irwin/McGraw-Hill

TM 12-2 Exhibit 12–3
Organizational and Interfunctional Factors Related to the Successful Implementation of Business Strategies

Organizational factor	Type of business strategy		
	Prospector	Differentiated defender	Low-cost defender
Functional competencies of the SBU	SBU will perform best on critical volume and share-growth dimensions when its functional strengths include marketing, sales, product R&D, and engineering.	SBU will perform best on critical ROI dimension when its functional strengths include sales, financial management and control, and those functions related to its differential advantage (e.g., marketing, product R&D).	SBU will perform best on critical ROI and cash flow dimensions when its functional strengths include process engineering, production, distribution, and financial management and control.
Resource allocation across functions	SBU will perform best on volume and share growth dimensions when percentage of sales spent on marketing, sales, and product R&D are high and when gross fixed assets per employee and percent of capacity utilization are low relative to competitors'.	SBU will perform best on the ROI dimension when percentage of sales spent on the salesforce, gross fixed assets per employee, percent of capacity utilization, and percentage of sales devoted to other functions related to the SBU's differential advantage are high relative to competitors'.	SBU will perform best on ROI and cash flow dimensions when marketing, sales, and product R&D expenses are low, but process R&D, fixed assets per employee, and percentage of capacity utilization are high relative to competitors'.
Decision-making influence and participation	SBU will perform best on volume and share-growth dimensions when managers from marketing, sales, product R&D, and engineering have substantial influence on unit's business and marketing strategy decisions.	SBU will perform best on ROI dimension when financial managers, controller, and managers of functions related to unit's differential advantage have substantial influence on business and marketing strategy decisions.	SBU will perform best on ROI and cash flow when controller, financial, and production managers have substantial influence on business and marketing strategy decisions.

(continues)

Irwin/McGraw-Hill

The McGraw-Hill Companies, Inc, 1999

Type of business strategy

Organizational factor	Prospector	Differentiated defender	Low-cost defender
SBU's organization structure	SBU will perform best on volume and share-growth dimensions when structure has low levels of formalization and centralization, but high level of specialization.	SBU will perform best on ROI dimension when structure has moderate levels of formalization, centralization, and specialization.	SBU will perform best on ROI and cash flow dimensions when structure has high levels of formalization and centralization, but low level of specialization.
Functional coordination and conflict resolution	SBU will experience high levels of interfunctional conflict; SBU will perform best on volume and share-growth dimensions when participative resolution mechanisms are used (e.g., product teams).	SBU will experience moderate levels of interfunctional conflict; SBU will perform best on ROI dimension when resolution is participative for issues related to differential advantage, but hierarchical for others (e.g., product managers, product improvement teams).	SBU will experience low levels of interfunctional conflict; SBU will perform best on ROI and cash flow dimensions when conflict resolution mechanisms are hierarchical (e.g., functional organization).

SOURCE: Adapted from Orville C. Walker, Jr., and Robert W. Rueckert, "Marketing's Role in the Implementation of Business Strategies," *Journal of Marketing*, July 1987, p. 31. Reprinted by permission from the American Marketing Association.

Irwin/McGraw-Hill

The McGraw-Hill Companies, Inc., 1999

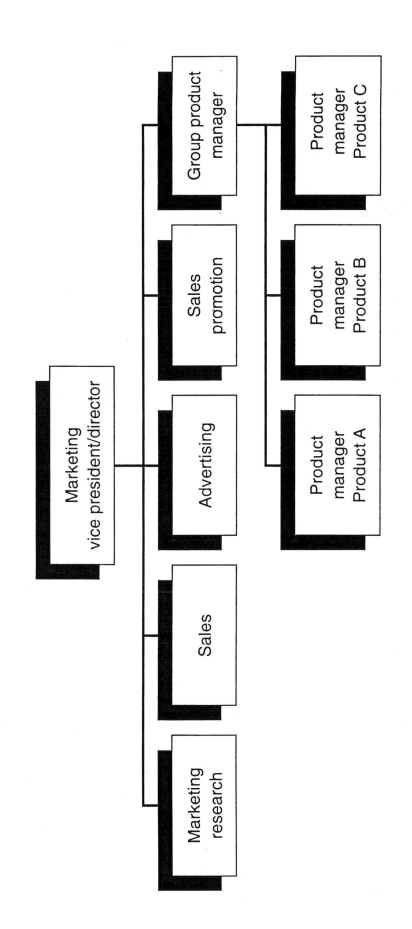

Section	Content
I. Executive summary	Presents a short overview of the issues, objectives, strategy, and actions incorporated in the plan and their expected outcomes for quick management review.
II. Current situation	Summarizes relevant background information on the market, competition, past performance of the product and the various elements of its marketing program (e.g., distribution, promotion, etc.), and trends in the macroenvironment.
III. Key issues	Identifies the main opportunities and threats to the product that the plan must deal with in the coming year and the relative strengths and weaknesses of the product and business unit that must be taken into account in facing those issues.
IV. Objectives	Specifies the goals to be accomplished in terms of sales volume, market share, and profit.
V. Marketing strategy	Summarizes the overall strategic approach that will be used to meet the plan's objectives.
VI. Action plans	This is the most critical section of the annual plan for helping to ensure effective implementation and coordination of activities across functional departments. It specifies • What specific actions are to be taken. • Who is responsible for each action. • When the action will be engaged in. • How much will be budgeted for each action.
VII. Projected profit-and-loss statement	Presents the expected financial payoff from the plan.
VIII. Controls	Discusses how the plan's progress will be monitored; may present contingency plans to be used if performance falls below expectations or the situation changes.

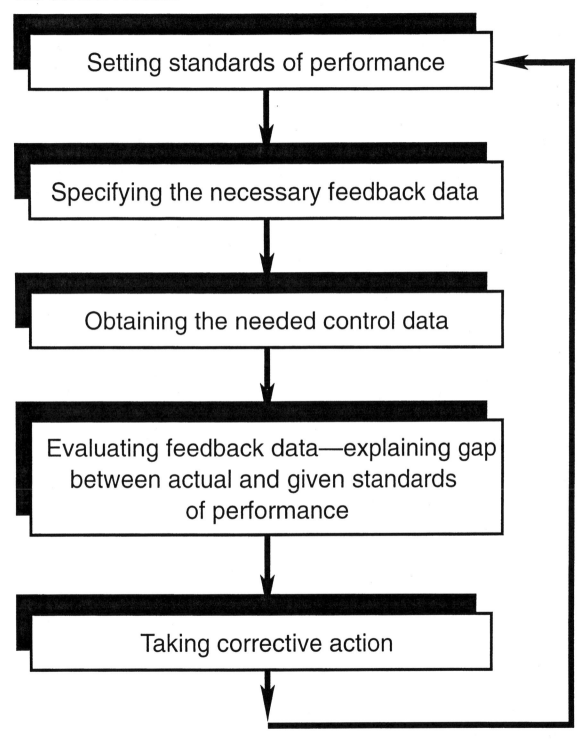

Setting standards of performance

Specifying the necessary feedback data

Obtaining the needed control data

Evaluating feedback data—explaining gap
between actual and given standards
of performance

Taking corrective action

Finding Product or Entry Profitability with Full Costing and Marginal Contributions Methods
(in $000s)

	Full costing	Marginal contribution
Net sales	$5,400	$5,400
Less: Cost of goods sold—includes direct costs (labor, material, and production overhead)*	3,800	3,800
Gross margin	$1,600	$1,600
Expenses		
Salesforce—includes direct costs (commissions) plus indirect costs (sales expenses, sales management overhead)†	510	450
Advertising—includes direct costs (media, production) plus indirect costs (management overhead)	215	185
Physical logistics—includes direct costs (transportation) plus indirect costs (order processing, warehousing costs)	225	190
Occupancy—includes direct costs (telephone) plus indirect costs (heat/air, insurance, taxes, building maintenance)	100	25
Management overhead—includes direct costs (product/brand manager and staff) plus indirect costs (salaries, expenses, occupancy costs of SBU's general management group)	180	100
Total	$1,230	$ 950
Profit before taxes	$ 370	
Contribution to fixed costs and profits		$ 650

*Production facilities dedicated to a single product.

† Multiproduct salesforce.

Irwin/McGraw-Hill

© *The McGraw-Hill Companies, Inc., 1999*

Effect of a $300,000 Increase in Sales Resulting from Increased Sales Commissions and Expenses of $35,000 (using same data as in Exhibit 13–4)

Net sales	$5,700
Less: direct costs (29.62%)	4,012
	$1,688
Expenses	
Sales commissions and expenses	485
Advertising	185
Physical logistics	190
Occupancy	25
Management	100
	$ 985
Contribution to overhead and profits	$ 703
Increase in profit (before tax) = $703 – $650 = $53	

© *The McGraw-Hill Companies, Inc., 1999*

Irwin/McGraw-Hill

Examples of Questions a Strategic Control System Should Be Able to Answer

1. What changes in the environment have negatively affected the current strategy (e.g., interest rates, government controls, or price changes in substitute products)?

2. What changes have major competitors made in their objectives and strategies?

3. What changes have occurred in the industry in such attributes as capacity, entry barriers, substitute products?

4. What new opportunities or threats have derived from changes in the environment, competitors' strategies, or the nature of the industry?

5. What changes have occurred in the industry's key success factors?

6. To what extent is the firm's current strategy consistent with the preceeding changes?

TM 13-5 Exhibit 13–8
Variance Decomposition Analysis

Market volume variance = actual (50,000,000) less planned (40,000,000) total market units × planned market share (50%)
= planned unit contribution (20¢)
= $1,000,000

Company volume variance = actual (22,000,000) less planned (20,000,000) units sold × planned unit contribution (20¢)
= $400,000

Company share variance = actual (44%) less planned (50%) × actual total units (50,000,000) × planned unit contribution (20¢) = $600,000

Contribution unit variance = actual (17.73¢) less planned (20¢) unit contribution × actual unit sales
= –$5,000,000

Total variance = market volume variance ($1,000,000) +
company volume variance ($400,000) +
company share variance (–$600,000) +
contribution unit variance (–$500,000) = $300,000

SOURCE: James M. Hulbert and Norman E. Toy, "A Strategic Framework for Marketing Control," *Journal of Marketing*, April 1977, pp. 12–20. Reprinted by permission of the American Marketing Association.

Irwin/McGraw-Hill

The McGraw-Hill Companies, Inc., 1999

TM 13-6 Exhibit 13–9
Sales Analysis Based on Selected Sales Territories

Sales territory	Salesperson	(1) Company sales 1997	(2) Sales quota 1997	(3) Overage, underage	(4) Percentage of potential performance
1	Barlow	$552,630	$585,206	−$32,576	94%
2	Burrows	470,912	452,800	+18,112	104
3	White	763,215	981,441	−218,226	77
4	Finch	287,184	297,000	−9,816	96
5	Brown	380,747	464,432	−83,685	82
6	Roberts	494,120	531,311	−37,191	93
7	Macini	316,592	329,783	−13,191	96

© *The McGraw-Hill Companies, Inc., 1999*

Irwin/McGraw-Hill

Non-Value-Adding Work Contents in a Hewlett-Packard Sales Region

Process	Percentage
Planning	0%
Product promotion	16
Customer search	28
Selling	35
Post-sales operation	62
Control	35
Total	35

Irwin/McGraw-Hill

Non-Value-Adding Work by Problem/Activity

Problem activity	Percentage
Incorrect deliveries	76%
Ineffective negotiations	31
Poor order processing	45
Incorrect quotations	43
Inconsequential demonstrations	66
Incorrect configurations	53
Ineffective relationship building	42
Wasted time with partners	41
Wasted traveling time	24
Ineffective communications	39

Irwin/McGraw-Hill

TM 13-9 Exhibit 13–12
Major Areas Covered in Marketing Audit and Questions Concerning Each for a Consumer Goods Company

Audit area	Examples of questions to be answered
Marketing environment	What opportunities and/or threats derive from the firm's present and future environment; that is, what technological, political, and social trends are significant? How will these trends affect the firm's target markets, competitors, and channel intermediaries? Which opportunities/threats emerge from within the firm?
Objectives and strategy	How logical are the company's objectives, given the more significant opportunities/threats and its relative resources? How valid is the firm's strategy, given the anticipated environment, including the actions of competitors?
Planning and control system	Does the firm have adequate and timely information about consumers' satisfaction with its products? With the actions of competitors? With the services of intermediaries?
Organization	Does the organization structure fit the evolving needs of the marketplace? Can it handle the planning needed at the individual product/brand level? Do good relations exist between sales and merchandising?
Marketing productivity	How profitable are each of the firm's products/brands? How effective are each of its major marketing activities?
Marketing functions	How well does the product line meet the line's objectives? How well do the products/brands meet the needs of the target markets? Does pricing reflect cross elasticities, experience effects, and relative costs? Is the product readily available? What is the level of retail stockouts? What percentage of large stores carries the firm's in-store displays? Is the salesforce large enough? Is the firm spending enough on advertising?

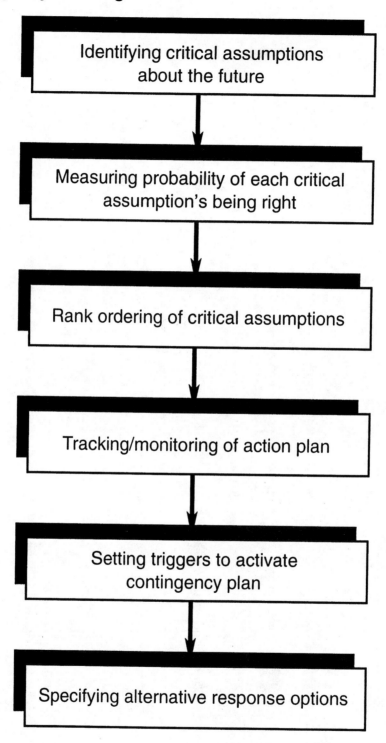